WELL SEASONED IN *Tuscany*

A YEAR IN THE LIFE

JENNIFER CRISWELL

GEMELLI PRESS

WELL SEASONED IN

Tuscany

A YEAR IN THE LIFE

Published by Gemelli Press LLC
9600 Stone Avenue North
Seattle, Washington 98103

Cover design and typesetting by Enterline Design Services

ISBN: 979-8-9863142-0-4
Library of Congress number pending

GEMELLI PRESS

For Marinella
My neighbor, my teacher, my friend

A Marinella.
La mia vicina in tutti i sensi della parola

PROLOGUE

When we last left our hapless yet plucky heroine (that would be me, of course) she'd finally received legal permission to work and had survived her first year in Tuscany.

Just.

It hadn't been all beguiling fruit vendors and frozen laundry, certainly, but I'd never imagined that realizing my dream would be quite so *faticoso*! In other words, exhausting.

Others had come before me and carved out satisfying lives in this beautiful country rich in the history of Leonardo and Dante. Theirs were tales of renovation and restoration amid the picturesque villages that pepper a luscious landscape of grapevines and olive groves.

But this was my journey. My mistakes to make and my victories to savor. I'd come with a desire to settle in the country of my ancestors and I'd thrown myself into the challenge wholeheartedly. I'd forged ahead with a brazen optimism and sense of adventure that was sometimes stymied but never stifled as I encountered stumbling blocks on my road to the sweet life. My mantra, *"At least you're in Tuscany,"* had gotten me through the tougher days. And there were definitely tough days. My mettle had been tested: I'd faced months of unemployment and belt-tightening, I'd flung myself through bureaucratic hoops like a Cirque du Soleil acrobat, and for a time I'd run more on gumption than actual hope of ever achieving my goal of becoming a citizen.

And then I got The Letter.

It was the end of December, sunny and crisp, two days before New Year's Eve, almost two years to the day that I had filed my application for Italian Citizenship. I was eligible for citizenship *jure sanguinis* thanks to my Sicilian great-grandparents, which basically meant that in addition to inheriting the best lasagne recipe in the world from Calogero and Emilia, I had also inherited through their bloodline the right to claim citizenship. As it turned out, learning to cook the sauce and assemble the lasagne had been a lot easier than navigating the citizenship process.

The letter was in Italian and came *raccomandata*, which in my experience was never good. It meant that instead of sending me an email, the *Comune* (town hall) had felt it necessary to spend money on an official, return-receipt requested letter that my post lady Angela hand-delivered. The last one I'd received in the spring had been two single-spaced pages of all but undecipherable Italian legalese. Really the only things I'd understood, aside from the signature of the mayor, were the Times Roman font and the word *rifiuto*, which signaled that my citizenship had been rejected based on a technicality that my Comune liaison Vania had foreseen. Her fancy footwork was the only reason I was still in the game.

The worst part of receiving these letters, other than the heart palpitations, cold sweat, and sense of doom, was having to rush over to my neighbor Marinella's house so she could confirm what I was reading. Her confirmation in the spring had driven me into a tailspin.

But this letter brought a different reaction. I still had the heart palpitations and cold sweat, but as I skimmed the letter, I felt a joyous sense of hope arise within me. They had kindly put into boldface type the important bit: "*Le è stato riconosciuto il possesso della cittadinanza italiana.*" You have been recognized as having Italian Citizenship.

I bit back a yelp. Still in shock, I called to Cinder, my aging and faithful Weimaraner, who was a constant source of reassurance as well as an intrepid cohort on my Tuscan adventure. She had been ambling some feet away, sniffing and marking her spots along our wet, bricked street, her nails click-clacking along as she nonchalantly edged toward a garbage bag with foul-smelling deliciousness spilling forth. Sensing my excitement, she about-faced and hastened to catch up as I practically skidded down the slippery path to Marinella's house. I hadn't bothered to grab a coat or even close our door. Her humongous, lovable Dalmatian mix, Ozzy, announced us before I could ring the bell. Marinella emerged, zipping up a wool cardigan.

"*Ma ti fa caldo?*" she asked with a smile as she opened the gate. Are you hot?

This was her motherly way of asking why in the heck I wasn't wearing a coat. It was a scene we'd played out on more than one occasion over the years.

"*Non importa.*" Never mind. I waved the letter. "I think I got my citizenship."

She grabbed her reading glasses from the gold chain looped around her neck and then scanned the letter. Her smile told me what I needed to know.

I GOT IT!!!

She clasped her hands together. "*Che bella notizia. Finalmente!*" Great news, finally. I beamed ear to ear, hugging her. I caught a familiar spicy scent of ragù; I'd obviously interrupted lunch preparations.

"*A dopo,*" she said gesturing toward the kitchen, already hurrying back inside. We'd talk later.

"*Grazie,*" I called to her, retreating backwards before skipping back home with Cinder.

And that was it. After the long, grueling months, the hundreds of pieces of paper that filled my citizenship binder, it was official. There had been no phone call from Vania, no hint that it was coming. It was almost anticlimactic. The words of Dr. Seuss popped into my head: "*It came without ribbons!... it came without tags!... it came without packages, boxes, or bags!*"

After poking my head in the fridge on the off chance that a bottle of prosecco might have magically materialized, I instead settled for a cup of mint tea and a *biscotto* to celebrate. I curled up on the couch and raised my cup to the photo of my great-grandparents. Was it a trick of the light or did their stern faces seem almost happy? I hoped one day I would make it to Sicily to see the town where they had met. It was comforting to think that they were watching out for me on my journey here.

I sipped my tea and thought of all the people I needed to share this news with including my mom and dad, everyone at work, and my friends in town. But for the moment I was still. I wanted to savor the good news. I had done it.

What I couldn't have known was that becoming Italian wasn't the end. Not even close. The lessons I'd learn as I put down roots in this community were just beginning.

I held my citizenship papers close to my chest and looked at Cinder who'd settled onto her bed, staring at me expectantly.

Now what?

PRIMAVERA

CHAPTER ONE

THE SECRET LIFE OF ASPARAGUS

My shoes sank and slurped into ground that was boggy after the heavy rains of winter. The April sun radiated strongly when it slyly peek-a-booed from behind heavy cloud cover. Giddy at the thought that winter was finally over, I breathed in the moist air, an earthy bouquet of sweet new grasses and musty vegetation. Small wildflowers poked out of sunny spots amid the trees.

Marinella and I were traipsing through an overgrown *bosco*, or woodland area, outside of Pienza in search of asparagus. And not just any asparagus mind you, but the elusive *asparagi selvatici*. Wild asparagus. Okay, so maybe they aren't so elusive if you know where to look; my personal asparagus-hunting guide professed expertise in sussing them out and optimistically had come armed with a small knife and basket.

In the time I'd known her, Marinella had gone from neighbor to friend, and then to close friend and motherly figure. I still had a good friendship with Antonella, who ran a grocery store in town, but I saw her infrequently, and so it was usually Marinella or expat friends Gill or Janet who fulfilled the role of confidant. Gill and Janet were my security blanket when I just needed to speak in my own language or laugh at another misstep in my adventure. Although we were *straniere* – a Brit, an Australian, and an American walk into a bar — we'd bonded through our common language and shared arsenal of cultural references.

My relationship with Marinella was different. She was a typical Tuscan mom. She was a bundle of energy who cared for two grown sons, a husband, one large dog, two parakeets, three turtles, and about six cats who'd cottoned on early that she was a soft touch. She had adopted me, another stray, as part of the family and looked out for me as if I were one of her own. When we were out together, people sometimes asked if I was her daughter. Since she didn't have a daughter to mother, our interactions often took on that dynamic. She was opinionated and bossy and was quite fond of telling me my mind. I'd mention that I had made a new acquaintance in town and she'd tell me I should stay away from them, or when I told her that my grandmother's lasagne recipe had ricotta in it she wrinkled her nose and insisted it wasn't lasagne. But she never took offense when I disagreed, and we had a comfortable rapport. I had relied on her counsel many times during that first difficult year and she had always been ready to lend an ear. From my ill-advised romance with Salvatore, the Sicilian fruit vendor, with resulting tears, she was always there. I supported her as well. I knew while she did everything for her boys, she felt unappreciated. She may have complained about the amount of laundry she had to do daily and the time it took to prepare their meals, but she wouldn't have had it any other way. She would have liked them in the nest forever. Seeing them with serious girlfriends and spending less and less time at home was difficult. If your job was to take care of everyone's needs, what did you do when they didn't need you anymore?

During my second year, when I had dropped off an Azalea plant for Mother's Day with a little thank you note for all of her support, Marinella's eyes had welled with tears. It was the first time I had ever seen her become emotional and it marked a turning point in our relationship. I had seen the smooth underbelly, and her willingness to be vulnerable cemented our bond.

She'd begun teaching me the recipes of Tuscany, and my favorite part of the week was spending time in her kitchen. She had taught me how to make her ragù, which I still think is the best I have ever tasted, and we'd spent a whole day on pasta. She had been patient as she'd demonstrated the proper way to hand roll the impossibly long ropes of *pici*, and a task master when showing me how thin the tagliatelle had to be before cutting it. They are still things I think about each time I make pasta on my own. In my kitchen in a place of honor is the traditional long rolling pin used for the tagliatelle. Marinella presented me the *mattarello*, or *ranzagnolo* as it is called locally, when I had mastered the pasta.

In the winter months when I wasn't working much, Marinella often proposed heading to the countryside for an afternoon walk, usually with Ozzy (Cinder was never invited because Ozzy didn't like other dogs in his car). Even if I wasn't in the mood for a walk, I always said yes; I still didn't have a car so any opportunity to explore the countryside outside the walls of Montepulciano was a treat. Our walks could be scenic and enjoyable, or with a specific intent in mind like hunting for mushrooms, or scary, like in January when we'd almost been mowed down by hunters looking for *cinghiale*, wild boar.

"What are they shouting about?" I'd asked nervously, as shotguns fired close by. Men with blaze-orange vests crashed through nearby underbrush. Others skirted past us on the dirt road speaking rapidly into walkie-talkies with a *Lord of the Flies*-esque fervor. So much noise while hunting seemed counterproductive, and I'd hoped the wild boar had scarpered.

"Hunters are crazy," Marinella had replied calmly, calling Ozzy back to us. "Let's head back toward the main road." Good idea. My friend Adrian had been winged by a hunter on his own property; it seemed a lot of *cacciatori* took the regulations to avoid shooting toward dwellings or roads as mere suggestion. Considering that Marinella and I both had dark auburn hair at that moment, odds were good that we were seconds away from being confused for cinghiale. I picked up the pace.

Thankfully, our asparagus outing proved to be more relaxing. Marinella was an old hand at scouring for wild edibles and showed me what to look for. I inspected the ground, trying to identify the fern-like foliage that announced the slender shoots. I found lots of cut foliage and trampled ferns but no asparagus. Someone had trod here before us. It seemed impossible, but it must be true. I scanned the distance looking for other cars. There were no signs or sounds of modernity. I could hear the gurgle of a fast-running stream nearby.

The grounds we were scouring abutted a monastery, *Monastero di Sant'Anna in Camprena*. The abbey was originally built in the 1300s as a hermitage for Benedictine monks.

This was one of my favorite parts of exploring the areas around the Val D'Orcia. You'd be walking in the countryside and come upon one of these ancient edifices that transported you immediately to another time. I'd become lost in my own thoughts envisioning pious monks meditating in their cells, cultivating their crops, or harvesting olive trees. What must it have been like to live so long ago? I occasionally still grumbled about hanging the laundry out to dry in the winter, and it was funny to me that I lit my stove with a match, but these certainly were not hardships.

Life in Tuscany had evolved into something I had never quite imagined. It was simple, the winters extremely quiet. Everything related to the seasons. It made sense, of course, since this was a land of farmers, but once I began experiencing each month by what chores needed be done and which bounties the earth had to offer, I began to see things in a different light. It's nature that dictates and provides. The result is that winter dishes can taste fresh and amazing like summer dishes because the tomatoes are put up in August when they are bursting from everyone's gardens. In the spring, baby artichokes are conserved under oil so they will be ready when their season finishes. And delicacies like wild asparagus will be found for just a few short weeks.

But of course it's not all about the food and wine. There are household conventions to follow, knowing when to have your shutters repainted and the correct time to buy your firewood. I learned so much just by watching the locals. Marinella had been obliging and helpful in all things related to food and cleaning.

"*Vieni qua,*" she beckoned me now. I hastened over to where she proudly held up one skinny stalk of asparagus.

"*Bello,*" I said approvingly, as I admired the spindly, delicate cousin of the asparagus I knew. I glanced at her basket. It was empty. She caught my eye and laughed.

"*Hanno già preso tutto*," Marinella said, shrugging pragmatically. They've already taken everything. Early bird gets the asparagus, apparently. We carried on for another hour, tramping through decaying leaves and over mossy rocks, before Marinella abandoned the cause and steered us toward an open field of wild grasses, *erbe spontanee*. She showed me how to seek out those to toss in a salad or add to a frittata. They looked like weeds. Or at best parsley. Squat little spirals that she identified, naming each variety. The only names I remembered were *dente di leone* so called because its leaves were shaped like lion's teeth (we know it as dandelion) and one that turned out to be the same exact plant but with a different nickname, *pisciacane*. Dog piss. Yummy!

"*Questo?*" I asked, pointing to a small clump that looked a sure bet for arugula.

She examined it for two seconds, chuckled and wagged her finger. "*Velenoso.*" Poisonous. The chuckle was because I had a knack for finding the poisonous varieties. The same thing happened when we had hunted for mushrooms. I sighed dramatically and Marinella continued to laugh.

Note to self, if ever lost in the woods . . . STARVE.

As we made our way back toward the car and the monastery, we came upon a small cemetery enclosed within an old stone wall. Its gates were rusted, its headstones ancient. A little stone chapel sat at one end and I walked slowly through its door, letting out a squeal as an object flew toward my head. Bats, I thought preparing to retreat, but then I looked more closely. I had disturbed some small brown swallows roosting in the eaves of the chapel. I smiled happily at them. Now it really was spring. The *rondini* were returning from the South. They were my touchstone.

As I exited the tiny church, I walked around the peaceful cemetery. It was cared for, the grass patchy but not overgrown. Some of the headstones were leaning, as if weary from standing vigilance for so many years. The place felt familiar, almost as if I had been here before.

"They made that film here," Marinella told me reading my mind. *Il Paziente Inglese.* Ahh. It had been many years since I had seen *The English Patient*, but that would explain the sense of familiarity. I glanced toward the monastery and its lofty bell tower flanked by a lane of stately cypresses. I could almost feel the melancholy in the air. This was where Juliette Binoche had cared for Ralph Fiennes.

I wandered down the path of cypresses, the iconic image of so many postcards of Tuscany. A few paces behind, Marinella called out potential suitors for me. This was a regular occurrence and while I did appreciate her dedication to finding me a mate, I had my doubts. I'd dated a couple of interesting Italians since my romance with Salvatore, but no one I would call a keeper. Admittedly, none of my dates had been suggested by Marinella so maybe I should start taking her recommendations more seriously. Left to my own devices, I clearly wasn't doing a stellar job.

Case in point, Salvatore, lead character in the aforementioned ill-advised romance. Part rogue, part sexy fruit vendor who'd acted as if he was divorcing his wife in Sicily, all the while pursuing me. And I'd fallen for him and his damn delicious peaches. As inadvisable as it may have been, my fling with Salvatore had been wildly romantic and a defining part of my first year in Italy.

When we arrived back at the car, Marinella displayed her bounty. A few clumps of lion's teeth/dog piss, and five asparagi. I had nothing to show for my efforts except for shoes that were soaked through and feet that were no doubt nicely pruned.

"*Prendili tu.*" Marinella said magnanimously offering me her basket. As much as I would have liked to try the wild asparagus, I declined. I attempted to translate "to the victor goes the spoils" into Italian but judging by Marinella's look of confusion I hadn't succeeded. My Italian was getting better, but it still needed work. I politely declined again. I knew she would whip up a fabulous frittata with the herbs and asparagus for her family. She'd taught me her frittata recipe and I made it often, always feeling satisfied when I successfully flipped it onto the plate and back into the pan without dripping egg all over the floor.

"*La prossima volta,*" I said, giving her a hug. It would mean waiting until next spring before we'd see the wild asparagus again, but that was okay. Besides

I had no doubt she was going to bring me a piece of frittata to sample anyway.

"*Ti porto un pezzettino*," Marinella declared, echoing my thoughts. I laughed. Marinella was also my touchstone. As dependable as the changing seasons.

CHAPTER TWO

TUESDAYS WITH MARI

Just days after the wild asparagus hunt, Cinder and I were heading for home after making short work of our morning walk. Spring had retreated and the prospect of pervasive damp gloom had me huddling in my coat, while Cinder stiffly double-timed her stride.

As we passed Marinella's gate, we heard the familiar squeak of her kitchen window opening. Ozzy rushed over, pushing his nose through the bars of the gate to touch noses with Cinder. She grudgingly accepted his kisses.

"*Faccio i pici oggi,*" Marinella called. "*Vieni?*" Today I am making *pici.* Are you coming?

Of course I would. I loved that Marinella didn't call or message. I didn't know if she even owned a cell phone. A greeting from the window worked just fine and was a welcome change from the constant pull of screen time on a smartphone.

But why *pici*? It was the first pasta Marinella had taught me and we had spent a lot of time rolling out those long, fat, spaghetti-like strands. Maybe she thought I needed the practice?

You quickly learn if you spend any amount of time in Italy that each region has a typical pasta, from the *orecchiette* in Puglia, to the *paccheri* in Campania, to the *trofie* in Liguria. In Tuscany, and specifically southern Tuscany, it's *pici*. You will find it on almost every restaurant menu, its long, strands cozying up to a *ragù*, or *bricioli* (breadcrumbs), or a sauce of *aglione*, a tomato sauce made with a large garlic variety that is sweeter and milder than its less kissable counterpart.

But you also find it at home. Almost every *nonna* I'd met in Montepulciano knew how to make *pici*.

I settled Cinder with a biscuit, grabbed my notebook, and headed next door.

I yelled a customary *"Permesso?"* before entering, which gives Italians warning that someone is entering their door. It's technically asking permission, but you're never denied. *"Sono in cucina,"* Marinella responded. I'm in the kitchen. Marinella wasn't a kiss-on-both-cheeks greeting kind of person, but the fact that she welcomed me into her house as a friend was much more meaningful to me than any perfunctory show of affection.

When I entered Marinella's kitchen I immediately felt a sensation of comfort. Cooking aromas are love, and a kitchen can evoke so many memories. The scent of my mom's banana bread just out of the oven was the aroma of my childhood. For some of my Italian friends it was a pot of bubbling ragù on a Sunday morning beckoning them to dip a piece of bread. Such a ragù greeted me now and my stomach gave an approving rumble in response to the rich tomatoey aroma.

Marinella's kitchen was the heart of the house, its beats could be felt in the scarred wood table that centered it, the dark walnut cabinets filled to capacity, her six-burner stove that never seemed to be without something simmering and wonderful on it, and an old black woodstove, its silver-handled ovens beckoning to be opened and filled with loaves of bread.

I positioned myself near the woodstove, warming my hands and letting the coziness of the space seep into me. One of the cats welcomed me by wending itself around my leg.

Marinella poured an espresso for each of us and we sipped for a minute in silence. When she finished and put on her red apron it would be time to start.

She told me we would be making the pasta for her niece, who had just given birth.

"Il tempo vola se siamo in due," she said. It will go faster if we do it together.

She added a crack about how my tagliatelle had improved, so now it was time to turn to improving my pici technique.

"Maybe I should quit while I'm ahead since the tagliatelle brought a tear to your eye," I told her.

She chuckled, "*Erano le allergie.*" It was allergies.

It was true that Marinella had gotten a little choked up when she saw how thin I had managed to roll the pasta sheet without ripping it. She'd spontaneously hugged me, although I was sure it had more to do with her happiness that someone was learning her recipes than with my proficiency.

Marinella often bemoaned the fact that the younger generation wasn't interested in learning traditional Tuscan recipes or maintaining the custom of working the land. She was convinced they were happier working in jobs with a steady paycheck like the post office or a bank.

Her own sons had no interest in the kitchen aside from bringing their appetites when they were called to the table. Maybe it would have been different if she'd had a daughter?

Marinella put on her red apron, tied the strings behind her back, then grabbed a bag of flour from the cabinet. I pulled out the big pasta board (*spianatoia*) that we would use to roll out the pici.

Marinella mixed the dough for the pasta, which was just flour and water, her practiced hands working the dough into a smooth round. It was almost imperceptible but did her normally assured movements seem labored?

When she finished, she inverted a bowl over the dough to let it rest. She leaned her weight on the table, which I had never seen her do before.

"*Stai bene?*" I asked. Are you okay?

"*Certo.*" Of course. But her furrowed brow belied her words.

Marinella's tone didn't invite further inquiry, but I resolved to keep an eye on her. She had been battling cancer for years, going in and out of remission and never seeming to miss a beat in her daily routine. Monthly visits to the doctor were unremarkable, and she seemed resigned to the poking and prodding. Fortunately, she'd been in remission since my first year living here and during that time had become an important person in my life. I didn't want to think about losing her.

I asked her if I could cut the pasta as I needed practice.

Marinella wordlessly handed me the knife.

As we worked, I tried to remember what she had taught me. Roll the strands with your whole hand not just your palm. The strands had to be quite long and thin, a bit fatter than spaghetti. I looked to Marinella to see if mine were thin enough. A quick nose wrinkle told me they were not. The last time we had done this together, she had said my strands looked like fat worms. Their offending pudginess had been accentuated when they were submerged in water.

Skinny worms, Skinny worms, I said to myself as I attempted to roll even longer thinner strands. Fabio, my colleague at Poliziano winery, would be impressed. He considered himself a *pici* expert. Fabio wasn't a trained chef but as Hospitality Manager he was tasked with preparing lunches for important clients. His lunches always garnered rave reviews, especially his ragù and his bruschetta.

Fabio didn't actually make *pici* himself, but he had a grandmother who had elevated *pici* making to an art form. She was able to roll with one hand and wind the continuous strand around her arm like it was yarn. It was amazing to see. If she would let herself be filmed, she would definitely become a YouTube sensation. Fabio's superpower was being able to identify *pici* that was made by hand versus that which had been made by machine and then reworked by hand. This was sometimes done in restaurants to mimic the uneven strands of hand rolled pasta. Fabio didn't get angry often but when he ordered handmade *pici*, paid for handmade *pici*, and then received reworked machine pasta, well let's just say you didn't want to mess with Fabio and his *pici*.

We gathered the strands into little nests so they could be portioned more easily and we put them on trays sprinkled with semolina flour to keep them from sticking.

When we had finished and I was getting ready to leave, Marinella spooned some ragù into a container and filled a plate with nests of *pici*.

"*Ora sei a posto per pranzo,*" Marinella said. Now you are all set for lunch.

"*Per molti pranzi! Grazie.*" I thanked her for setting me up with many lunches and gave her a quick hug with my free arm.

Later as I reheated some ragù and put water on to boil for lunch, I felt slightly guilty that I was taking *pici* away from Marinella's niece, but thankfully this thought was subsumed by a more pressing one.

One nest or two?

CHAPTER THREE

TALES FROM THE TASTING ROOM

"This is Asinone," I told the young, fresh-faced, newlyweds from Kansas, presenting a bottle of Vino Nobile to them. I'd just taken them on a tour of the winery, and now Chuck and Leanne were seated at a long, rustic, wooden table, tasting some of Poliziano's best wines. On this grey, drizzly day, the tasting room was warm and inviting. Fabio had called me a few days before to say we had some bookings. I resisted the urge to shout "Hallelujah!" but I was more than ready to don my polyester blend, Poliziano polo shirt and get back to it. Seasonal work meant downtime in the winter and it wasn't easy to make ends meet in those five long months without a paycheck.

When I'd let Marinella know that I was starting back to work she'd generously offered to look in on Cinder like she had the last season. I was extremely grateful for the help.

Although the day was unseasonably gray, the vines outside our tasting room had benefitted from some strong sunshine in March and now were showing their first shoots. It was remarkable to see the evolution of the vines each year, from bud break, to flowering, to the first fruit setting. Each day as I began tours in the vineyard, I felt such a connection to nature. I hoped the visitors who came through felt it too.

I served the newlyweds a generous pour of Asinone as I introduced them to the rich, full-bodied perfection of my favorite wine.

The atmosphere had become increasingly awkward, so I'd tapered off my visits and now I usually just made my espresso at home. I felt the loss of our familiar routine and Serena's company, and I know Cinder felt the loss of all of those brioche scraps.

On this particular morning after our outing, I left Cinder to her morning ablution of chest licking (a strange new habit she'd no doubt picked up from Marinella's cats), made myself presentable, and headed into town. I needed to get a dress for Stefano's wedding. If I wasn't a tall, Amazonian American this might have been a simpler task, but I always found shopping in Italy a bit torturous. First there was the constant doubt if I was buying something suitable for the occasion. For fancier events the women here often seemed to dress as if they were going to a nightclub, lots of black and spangles and sparkly stuff. So, I wasn't really sure what was appropriate for a morning wedding. The next problem would be shoe shopping. The shoe shops typically would carry one pair of shoes in my size, or my number as they called it here. And well my number was 41 (An American size 10). Usually when I asked for a 41, I would just get sad head shaking as if I were suffering from some sort of affliction.

Despite its shopping challenges, Montepulciano hadn't lost its charm for me. The medieval walls, ancient brick buildings, narrow passages, Etruscan tombs, and the comforting chime of church bells all still held a magical, fairytale-like quality. The old *palazzi* seemed to reverberate with the history of lives lived.

It now felt like home.

I strolled up the cobbled street of the main *corso*. A playful sunshine spilled joyfully out of nooks and crannies along the street and brought a welcome heat that had had been missing from the winter's insipid rays. I stepped aside as a group of Nordic tourists trailing their guide marched briskly up the corso, pointing to shops that they would no doubt frequent after their tour was done. Montepulciano was a tourist town and in another month it would be bursting with visitors coming to sample its Vino Nobile or take in the ancient edifices. I loved the bustle during the summer but the tranquil weekends of spring were also precious.

I waved and smiled at Marisa in the lingerie shop, slightly ahead of the season sorting a new arrival of bathing suits, and at Luisa whose family ran the *erboristeria* and who was displaying some handmade jewelry outside the shop.

While much of the town remained the same, some things had changed in the four years I'd lived here. Shops had come and gone. I glanced wistfully at the spot that had housed my bread shop (*forno*). The family that owned it hadn't been from Montepulciano, and they'd never managed to win over the locals. While I appreciated that my neighbors were loyal to the entrenched establishments, I keenly felt the loss of my delicious whole-wheat loaves and the jolly, heavyset woman who'd sold them. I understand patronage, but the bakery owners had been from nearby Pienza, not (gasp) France or something.

I didn't like to frequent the other *forno* because it was next to the house of my first landlady, Luciana, and I had no desire to run into her. We always greeted each other with a chilly head nod if we crossed paths at the market, but I had left her overpriced, mold-ridden apartment without a backward glance. My new apartment was a bit lacking in modern amenities but lighting my stove with a match was a small price to pay to be free of Luciana.

I passed the butcher shop and although I saw Marinella standing at the counter, I didn't go in. Silvano was holding court. The local butcher, Silvano had a penchant for gossip and was no doubt making mince of someone's personal life, even as he wrapped up steaks and chops. Having been on the receiving end of Silvano's skewers in the past, I preferred to get my meat from the Conad supermarket, without the side of snark.

I stopped in to Cugusi, my favorite cheese shop, to pick up Fabio's cheese order for our tasting room since their delivery van had broken down. It gave me a chance to say hello to Caterina and to indulge my latest cheese obsession, *pecorino gran riserva*. Sharp and persistent, it was aged eighteen months, had a crumbly texture like *parmigiano*, and finished with a lingering nutty sweetness– lovely after work with a glass of Vino Nobile, or with crackers and a dollop of red pepper jelly.

Caterina greeted me with a smile as she rang up an elderly woman's ricotta.

"You're a good mom. When I come to live at your house, I'll be sure to give you all my mending." Antonella laughed and then snapped the thread with her teeth as she finished her work.

It was a running joke between us that I would someday rent the apartment that Antonella had below her house. She lived near my friend Laura's *agriturismo* (bed & breakfast on a working farm) in the countryside a few kilometers from town. Marinella and I went out that way often for our walks. The two-bedroom apartment had a separate entrance, a fireplace, and a gorgeous view of Montepulciano. She'd even promised me a little plot for a garden so I could grow the two things I could never find here, cilantro and sweet potatoes. Never mind that I killed most plants that came under my care, I doggedly held onto my unrealistic but attractive vision of myself living off the land ala Scarlett O'Hara clutching that carrot.

The only fly in the ointment of my plan was how to get there.

"Laugh," I told Antonella, "but I am getting a car this year if it kills me."

As much as I enjoyed living near Marinella and Janet in town, my dream was to live in the countryside. It seemed wrong somehow that after working ten hours a day, when I returned home to my apartment that I had no outdoor space. My view was delightful, but unless I was prepared to hang out the window with my glass of wine, my options for enjoying it were limited. I'd become an odd fixture I am sure, sitting with Cinder in the asphalted parking area near my house pretending that it was my yard and watching the sunset.

If I wanted to slap mosquitoes in the privacy of my own garden while eating cilantro-laden guacamole, I first needed to save enough money to get a car.

No problem, right?

I left Antonella and popped into Fatamorgana, a boutique I adored, to see if there was anything appropriate for a June wedding. I found lots of lovely things. Lovely expensive things.

Save for car? Dress for wedding?

After trying on half a dozen options, I settled on a pretty sundress with a wrap, not my first choice, but within my budget. I went directly home with my purchases before I could be tempted by all the beautiful summer sandals on display in shop windows. I grabbed Cinder, a book, and my beach chair and headed over to the parking area to enjoy my day off. The day was sunny and the scent of blooming *ginestra* (Scotch broom) perfumed the air. I tilted my faced toward the sun.

It wasn't perfect, but it was home.

CHAPTER FIVE

PRIMO DI MAGGIO

Atantalizing aroma of sweet, candied nuts mingled with savory roasted *porchetta*, signaling that Montepulciano's annual fair was setting up. Despite being just down the street from my apartment, the vendors had been stealthy in their approach and I hadn't heard them arriving. But as Cinder and I greeted a day of cloudless skies and warm spring sunshine, a buzz of activity broke the morning silence. Our street was already blocked off to traffic.

The sense of anticipation was palpable. Awnings unfurled as seasoned vendors chatted or munched on *panini*, setting out their wares with ballet-like precision. I could now recognize accents from other parts of Italy, enjoying the sing-songy musicality of the north contrasting with the more raspy tones of the south. We ambled past the stall where my Australian friend Janet bought her colorful linen dresses each year, the housewares truck with its impressive selection of pots, frying pans, and utensils, and headed further into the crush of trailers lining the road outside the town's main gate and spilling into the park. I wanted to check out the plant vendors. They were usually about halfway down the hill near the supermarket. The fair stretched from Sant'Agostino church inside the walls, all the way down to the bus station, where the bells, whistles, and flashing lights of a carnival would soon delight with cotton candy, rides, and games for the kids.

There were no crowds this early, but later in the day it would be like being caught in a rip current of people. You needed to determinedly change direction or risk being swept along.

It was official; it was the first of May.

Holidays abound in Italy. Aside from the biggies — public holidays like New Year's, Easter Monday, and Christmas — there are also lesser-known celebrations during the summer months, which continually vex visitors unable to figure out why everything is closed. The principal one on August 15th is *Ferragosto,* which in ancient times was a rest period after the heavy labor of summer and before the harvest. Now it's the period when Italians take their long summer holidays so you'll find lots of shops closed, beaches packed, and signs declaring that business will resume in September. Sometimes the signs say "maybe," which I guess gives them the option not to return if they are having a really good time. People scramble to close on properties, finish home repairs, or attend to their banking needs before everything shuts down or businesses shrink to skeletal staff.

The holidays most often skimmed over in the tour guides are the second of June, *Festa della Repubblica,* which commemorates Italy's voting to become a republic in 1946 after the fall of fascism, and *Primo di Maggio,* the first of May.

Primo di Maggio is the International Worker's Day, also called *Festa del Lavoro* and its origins are linked to Labor Day in the United States, which although celebrated in September was actually in response to the labor demonstration and resulting Haymarket massacre in Chicago in the first days of May, 1886.

In Italy, many towns celebrate May 1 with a local fair. My first year living here, also known as THE YEAR of TERRIBLE COMPREHENSION, when people told me that the first of May was a *"festa del lavoro"* I just thought they meant they got a day off for the fair. Oops.

Montepulciano's fair, also known as *Fiera di Sant'Agnese,* is well-known throughout the province of Siena and it's a day of excitement and celebration. The festivities begin in the morning with a historic procession (*corteo*) originating at the church of Sant'Agnese. Sant'Agnese is the patron saint of Montepulciano and her remains, which are thought to have brought healing miracles to many people, still rest in the church. Her right foot is raised in the air because as the story goes when Santa Caterina came to venerate the relics she bent to kiss the foot of Sant'Agnese and it lifted, thus renewing the belief in healing miracles.

The *corteo* winds its way from the church's sanctuary up to Piazza Grande. It flows through each district or *contrada* of the town, with each contrada represented by a king and queen, flag throwers, and drummers all in full medieval dress. It is the official opening of the season *Contradaiolo*. The morning ceremonies are followed by thousands of people descending on the town to seek out goods from over three-hundred vendors who come from all over Italy.

I liked to get out early to buy basil plants for my windowsill before they were picked over by the crowds. Also, it was impossible to bring Cinder around later in the day with so many people. Even now, she yanked me hard in the direction of a discarded scrap of pizza that lay in wait.

As I passed Sant'Agnese church, a few people milled about in medieval regalia, waiting for the morning processional to begin.

Further on, I spotted a vendor with garden plants and wished, not for the first time, that my plant lady, Nadia, participated in the annual fair. She and my fruit vendor Salvatore never joined the chaos of *Primo di Maggio*, preferring instead to just work the regular Thursday market. I had seen both of them this week on my way to work. I'll admit to being slightly spoiled. Even though Salvatore had been demoted from love interest to good friend, he still insisted on calling out "*Alta, bella, Americana*," whenever he saw me, and on honoring my three euro a week rate for all the fruits and veggies I could carry. During the winter when things were lean, this generosity was a huge help. And in the spring when I had to get on a bus in the mornings, I cheerfully schlepped bags of artichokes, fava beans, eggplant, arugula, asparagus, and blood oranges to work with me.

Nadia had also become a friend, making sure I never wanted for fresh-cut flowers in my life. She and her husband Alberto lived a few hours away, and like Salvatore they traveled around to the local markets, selling a beautiful array of plants and cut flowers.

Nadia was from Florence and knew a little German and English. She'd been patient with me when I'd been struggling with the language and often dazzled with an impressive knowledge of plant names in both English and Italian. She wore her hair in a tight ponytail, its unruly strands of salt and pepper curls usually attempting to spring free. Her smile was the same. Even when she had moments of seriousness, a smile seemed to lurk just below the surface waiting to emerge. She had a playful relationship with her husband Alberto, who was fond of bantering with Nadia as well as with the clients.

"*Mi raccomando*," he said to me teasingly almost every week as I departed with my purchases. Behave!

A powerfully built, handsome Italian, Alberto kept a wad of cash in his pocket to make change for customers and a cigar in hand. While Nadia spent the morning selling flowers, Alberto could usually be found two stands over chatting and smoking with one of his pals. When she needed help, Nadia's shouts of "ALBERTO!" would then be echoed by Salvatore's booming baritone at the next stand until Alberto would reluctantly return to assist some elderly matron with her flat of geraniums.

When I'd seen Nadia this past Thursday, I had just added a bunch of tangerine gerbera daisies to my already overflowing bag of veggies, when she'd told me to wait. Rooting around in her selection of seeds, she'd grabbed a packet.

"*L'ho trovato*," she'd told me, waving the packet in the air and handing it to me with a flourish. "*Divertiti*!" I found it, enjoy!

I'd glanced first at the photo of the cilantro foliage before reading *Coriandolo*! I grinned.

"*Che meraviglia*! I can't believe you found it." I'd been searching high and low for cilantro seeds for years but none of the local nurseries or vendors, including the ones at the fair, stocked them. It wasn't an herb the Italians used in their cooking (this could be in part because they thought the fragrance of cilantro was similar to the odor given off by the stink bugs often found clinging to curtains at the end of summer) so the fact that Nadia had persisted in her attempts to find the seeds made them all the more special.

I hugged her, already planning to add the fresh leafiness to my homemade salsa in the summer.

"Have Marinella help you with them," she said, her aquamarine eyes twinkling merrily. Nadia knew all too well how terrible I was with plants. It never stopped me from buying them, but Marinella's garden had become a refuge for all the plants I'd homed and then later took to her for rehabilitation.

"*D'accordo,*" I said laughing. Agreed. "It's the only way they'll have fighting chance at survival."

Now as I bought two healthy basil plants from a vendor I remembered from the year before but who didn't remember me, I appreciated again the beauty of living in a small town where you had relationships with the local people and their products.

I scouted a few stands that had table linens and sandals but decided I would wait for Janet for any important purchases. We usually did a round together after lunch.

As if on cue, Cinder pulled me toward a bright yellow food truck that we knew well. The words "Rosticceria Volante" were written in script on one side.

"Ciao Zio Angelo," I said cheekily after we'd waited our turn. Angelo was the uncle of one of my English students, Alessio. Alessio had begun lessons with me at seven years old and was now ten. He and his best friend Paolo were two of my best students, getting the highest marks in their class and insisting on lessons even during school holidays.

Flaming orange hair was an identifying feature in Alessio's family, but Zio Angelo hadn't gotten the memo; spikes of brown hair poked out from beneath a baseball cap. During one of our lessons, Alessio had proudly told me (in English) of his uncle's truck, which sold "the best chicken" at the market. Cinder and I had become frequent customers.

I ordered a roasted chicken, managing to resist the seductive scent of fried zucchini and potato croquettes. I struggled with Cinder who danced impatiently at my side, her nails clicking madly.

Zio Angelo winked at me, then shoved some of the battered, fried zucchini into a brown bag and put them in with my order.

"*Mi stai ammazzando,*" I told him with an exaggerated sigh. You're killing me. He laughed.

I shook my head in resignation as I thanked him and assured him we'd see him the next week.

Already laden with too much, I stopped one last time to add a basket of strawberries to my burden. Strawberries and roast chicken would definitely cancel out the fatty deliciousness of fried zucchini, right?

We made our way home accompanied by the rhythmic boom of drums as the processional began slowly snaking its way up the corso.

+ + +

Cinder, her belly now sated with chicken, dozed contentedly in a patch of afternoon sunlight as I struck out to meet Janet for another lap around the fair.

Janet and her husband Ken had become family to me. Aside from wonderful Sunday lunches filled with roasts, wine, *vin santo*, and conversation, we also shared a closeness because of our foreignness. We could laugh at the predicaments we encountered with the language and commiserate when things didn't always go to plan. Despite having lived here for over twenty-five years, Ken didn't speak much Italian and relied on Janet to get them through. A dapper Englishman, almost twenty years Janet's senior, Ken was first and foremost an artist. He'd gone from art director at major advertising agencies in New York and Sydney to enjoying his retirement in Italy. You could usually find him tucked up in his attic studio, whistling a melancholy tune and capturing the beauty of Montepulciano with his paintbrush.

Janet was another story. Despite having lived here for so many years, Janet didn't think of Italy as home. She'd come here for Ken and while she didn't regret that decision, she'd had her struggles here just as I had. We saw each other frequently, often just the two of us, sharing moments of girl time over tea and biscuits or a large glass of wine. She drove me nuts at times because, like Marinella, she was bossy and fond of telling me the "right" way to do things. I loved her despite this tendency and was now comfortable enough that I could tell her to stop whenever it got to be too much.

As I approached Janet's house, she emerged wearing a cardigan, which coordinated with her favorite red patent leather pumps. She locked the door and tucked her keys into the pocket of beige woolen trousers. She never carried a purse to the fair because she was wary of pickpockets in the crowds.

"Hello, possum!" She smiled widely and bussed me on both cheeks. "Are we ready to shop?"

"Always."

We made our way through the throng of people who'd amassed near the main gate and tried to weave our way down the street.

"Did you get Ken his porchetta?" I asked as we paused to dig through the colorful piles of linen I'd seen earlier. I was forever buying tablecloths for some reason. As much as I hated to iron, I loved having cheerful table linens. I decided on one with tiny checks of crimson and white and then contemplated a colorful throw for the couch.

"Yes, it wouldn't be the fair without it. I know we can buy the porchetta every week at the market, but we like the treat of having it just once a year. Plus this vendor's pork seems to be less salty for some reason than the Thursday ones." I nodded in understanding. I usually avoided the porchetta from the market because even if it was delicious, the herb stuffing was overly salted.

We made our way the length of the fair chatting and catching up on our week, occasionally waving or stopping to greet people we knew. I used to feel self-conscious whenever Janet and I spoke in English because the Italians would stare at us as if we were exotic animals at the zoo, but now I didn't mind. It was like having our own secret language.

I tried on sandals and bought a new hoodie, while Janet opted for socks and knickers. Then we spotted our favorite truck and made a beeline to stock up on the dried fruits and nuts we couldn't find locally at the Conad supermarket.

The sun was strong with the promise of hot summer days ahead. I turned my head toward the warmth and basked a little as the vendor from the south of Italy scooped up my dried cranberries and walnuts.

"They are going to offer the sommelier course here this

winter," Janet told me after she finished ordering candied ginger, orange peel, currants, and other dried fruits she'd use for making mince pies during the holidays. I'd ask Antonella to vacuum pack everything for us so they would last until needed.

My ears perked up at the word sommelier.

"Great . . . if it happens. Marco has been promising that for two years and in the end they never choose Montepulciano." Janet didn't have a car either and so we'd both been waiting for the FISAR (*Federazione Italiana Sommelier Albergatori Ristoratori*) course to be offered here, and not forty minutes away in Chiusi. My colleague Marco, aside from being a phenomenal sommelier, now taught a lesson or two of the course. He'd encouraged me to sign up. Because of my work at Poliziano, I'd gone from wine drinker to having a real, ahem, thirst for learning about the process, so I was definitely ready to take things to the next level. Janet offered walking tours of the town and worked with the *Strada del Vino Nobile* in the summer translating for their weekly tasting event, so for her, too, it would be a useful accreditation to have.

"I hope it happens," she said, as we made our way back up the hill with our treasures. "I have been getting more and more requests for wine tours."

"I'll start saving my pennies, just in case," I said. "Let's hope our Italian is good enough to understand what the heck they are saying in class."

"Don't be silly. That's why God invented wine," Janet said. "Even if we embarrass ourselves, we'll be tasting three or four wines each week so we won't notice."

"Speaking of wine," she concluded as we neared our street, "After you check on Cinder, come for a glass. Ken should be ready for a break and we'll open some fizz."

I smiled as I headed home. The fair and an afternoon glass of prosecco. The season had officially begun.

Marinella's Frittata

- Zucchini (one large or two small)
- 4 eggs (beaten)
- olive oil
- salt and pepper
- parmesan reggiano (optional)

(I use pecorino because it's what I usually have)

Wash, then chop zucchini into cubes and, over medium flame, saute in olive oil (best quality) until tender. I don't measure the oil, but use enough so that when you add the eggs, they won't stick to the pan. Season the zucchini to taste. Add the eggs. I turn the heat down to medium low at this point as the eggs are cooking. Grate some cheese over the eggs. Cook until the sides begin to pull away from the pan a bit. It's important that it not be "wet" when you flip it onto the plate, so just cook it until you think it's ready. (*Sorry these may be the worst directions ever!*) When ready to finish it, flip it onto a plate and then slide it back into the pan on its opposite side. Cook for another minute or two and then you are done!

ESTATE / SUMMER

"*No, da Salvatore. É troppo presto per i miei.*" They were from Salvatore; it was too early for hers.

She arched a brow. "*Che cosa hai preso TU da Salvatore?*" What did YOU get from Salvatore?

I laughed. "*Niente. Anche se lui prova sempre. Ma ho preso solo la frutta, ti giuro.*" Nothing, even if he always tries. I just got fruit and vegetables, I swear.

It was Salvatore's last market for the summer. He was now on his way to Sicily to work in his citrus orchards. We wouldn't see him again until September.

"*Ora devo comprare la frutta per tre mese. Che tristezza.*" I sighed dramatically. Now I have to buy my fruit for three months. How tragic!

"*Scema,*" Marinella chuckled. Idiot.

Fried zucchini flowers were the perfect *aperitivo* (appetizer) food, and at this time of year a glass of cold prosecco and a hot, salty zucchini flower was a delicious pairing. Sometimes at a bar they came stuffed with mozzarella and piece of anchovy, or even ricotta. Marinella, however, was a purist so we were making them unstuffed. Her batter was light with just flour, egg, and sparkling water.

As we dredged the prepared blossoms in the batter and then placed them in the hot oil, I prepared a plate with paper towels to rest the finished flowers and sprinkle them with salt.

The scent of fried zucchini flowers drew Marinella's husband Nicola into the kitchen.

"*Si puo?*" he asked looking hopefully at the plate of flowers.

"*Certo,*" Marinella told him, watching as he grabbed a hot flower, blowing on it before biting into it.

"*Complimenti. Molto buono.*" Really good.

Marinella and I each tasted one too. Delicious.

"*Questo è pranzo oggi,*" Marinella declared. Lorenzo and Giacomo were away for the weekend so apparently Marinella was not planning on cooking (beyond this frying, of course).

Nicola nodded in agreement. "*Perfetto, si fa così.*" He began rummaging in the refrigerator, pulling out salami, a package of prosciutto, some pecorino, and a bottle of prosecco.

"*Pranzi con noi, vero?*" Marinella said. You'll stay for lunch, right?

"*Volentieri.*" With pleasure.

I helped Nicola set the table, while Marinella cleaned up the remains of our cooking lesson. I unwrapped the deli paper and plated the prosciutto; Nicola sliced the cheese and salami. Marinella reached into a cabinet and pulled out a jar of baby artichokes that she'd put up just the month before. They were Lorenzo's favorite so they never lasted long. She added it to our makeshift picnic.

We sipped prosecco while we ate and talked about summer. Marinella had plans to pull out the lavender plants in the courtyard. I knew she was serious because she'd already organized with the Comune to cut down her huge pine tree to use in the town square for Christmas. The lavender plants were next on the chopping block because they were unruly and threatening to take over the planters. I loved the lavender, not only the gorgeous fragrance, but also the untamed look it gave to the garden.

I pleaded with her to leave the lavender because it's so beautiful, but Marinella would not be swayed. As she started to rise to make the coffee, Nicola put a hand on her shoulder.

"*Ci penso io,*" he promised, referring to the lavender. I'll take care of it. And sure enough by the next week he'd pulled out all of the lavender, and Marinella wasted no time in redoing the planters with pink hydrangeas, which were more orderly perennials.

We took our coffee in the courtyard. The day was perfectly sunny and warm with the promise of summer. I recounted some of the highlights of my work week at the winery including a lady from Minnesota who had stolen Fabio's cheese.

I'd just brought the Minnesota group a plate of pecorino gran riserva to pair with their last wine, Asinone. The group was a little loud but a lot of fun.

As I was heading back to the kitchen, one of the women from the Minnesota group came rushing out of it. Her cheeks were bulging like a squirrel full of winter nuts. Fabio was hot on her heels. He grabbed me by the arm and pulled me into the kitchen.

"She stole our cheese. *Tutto!*" All of it. Fabio's voice rose to a falsetto. He wildly gestured toward the workbench where I'd left a good-sized wedge of the gran riserva. It had been devastated. A few uneven crumbs remained. "She said she was looking for the bathroom. But she ate it all. *Tutto tutto tutto.*"

I had never seen Fabio look so flummoxed, and you knew it was serious by the word repetition. He couldn't conceive of a world where a person could violate his kitchen like this. My shoulders started to heave with laughter. I mimicked his reaction. "*Tutto!*" All of it.

"Laugh, but these are your people." Fabio tried to look stern but he began laughing too.

"Yes, I know. We are cheese-thieving lunatics."

In the end, all was forgiven in Fabio's eyes because the group sent home a few cases of wine, but the woman avoided eye contact with me for the rest of the tasting.

Both Nicola and Marinella laughed appreciatively throughout my tale, particularly my impression of Minnesota lady with her cheeks stuffed full of cheese.

Nicola excused himself, heading upstairs for his afternoon *riposino* (nap). Marinella walked me to the gate, telling me that she would watch Cinder while I was at the wedding the next Saturday, and that she expected a full report.

"*Assolutamente,*" I promised. Absolutely.

As I walked home, I felt a little pang of nervousness about experiencing a new social situation. This was nothing new for me. Life in Italy had been a series of walking into unknown scenarios and then flying by the seat of my pants. While I was looking forward to Stefano's wedding, often there was a learning curve with Italian traditions. It was easy to put a foot wrong. And I'm not talking about innocent cultural offenses like drinking a cappuccino after dinner or driving the speed limit. I just didn't want to end up like the expat who had been ostracized by her Italian friends because she'd opened a bottle of champagne on New Year's Eve and drank a glass before midnight. It was a cautionary tale.

Given that my only experience with Italian weddings was limited to film and even then only a vague memory of the nuptials in *The Godfather*, where animated family members danced the *tarantella* and sang "*Cè La Luna Mezzo Mare*," I probably should have asked friends what to expect.

But then again, why buck tradition?

CHAPTER SEVEN

IL MATRIMONIO / THE WEDDING

The day of the wedding, my escorts, Fabio and Marco, picked me up at 10:30 in the morning. That should have been my first clue that this was not going to be like the weddings I knew from the States. The invitation had indicated that the wedding started at that hour so I just figured it was *de rigueur* to be fashionably late. But then we stopped at a bar for coffee. Always compulsively early for everything, I began to get anxious as the boys casually sipped espresso and had a chinwag about the private lives of mutual acquaintances. Heaven knows what they said about me when I wasn't around.

I suppressed a groan as one of our youngest colleagues, Mattia, entered the bar looking like a kid playing dress up with his powder blue suit and slicked-back hair.

"*Mitico*," Fabio said, slapping him on the back. *Mitico* means myth and the Italians use it in the sense of "the man, the myth, the legend." I hoped he was using the term ironically. Mattia was not my favorite person. He was young, about twenty-two, and considered the computer whiz kid of Poliziano. In other words, he knew how to book airline tickets and do basic computer tasks that were beyond the skill set of the rest of the office. In the summers when I had to walk fifteen minutes from the bus stop to the winery each day, Mattia zoomed past me every morning in his shiny red Alfa Romeo without offering me a ride. Every other person who worked at the winery stopped to offer me a lift if they

My friend Tiziana sat nearby with her crew of ladies from the warehouse and bottling area. They were all laughing and looked to be having a great time.

Fabio, who was seated across from me, caught my eye and mouthed, "The fun table."

I grinned, gesturing toward Mattia and Stefania who were sitting to his right talking about work. We raised our glasses in a conspiratorial toast. I really hoped our table would loosen up a bit.

What followed was a flurry of food. Delicate aromas of seafood from the *insalatina di mare* (seafood salad) were quickly subsumed by the heady aroma of fried fish emanating from the kitchen, no doubt from the *spiedini di gamberoni e frittura* (skewers of fried shrimp and fish). Elegantly attired waiters brought out plate after plate. Then they'd return in what seemed like only a few minutes with platters loaded with seconds, their serving forks and spoons wielded expertly, as they encouraged us to have a bit more. It was decadent and delicious, a feast for the eyes as well as the stomach. It wasn't rushed, just constant.

Bottles of wine flowed freely so the mood relaxed and I listened to amusing stories that had occurred before my time as I nibbled on a piece of marinated octopus.

"We have had some fun moments in the tasting room too, right, Criswell?" The table's attention shifted to Fabio. I was curious as to which story he would recount: The woman who acted out a *When Harry Met Sally* fake orgasm when she tasted one of the tomatoes from Fabio's bruschetta, or the one with the woman and the vibrating table. It would definitely be one of those.

"So we had this group from Chicago. All women," Fabio began. Vibrating table for the win. "They were already drunk when they arrived. I was explaining how we sort the grapes on a vibrating table when one of the women launched herself at me across the table. Fabio mimicked the woman leering at him and slurring, "Is it only the fruit that gets to ride on the vibrating table?"

I chimed in. "Fabio's discomfort at that moment was incredible as he slowly comprehended what she meant. He beat a hasty retreat." The table erupted in laughter.

Fabio winked at me. Yes, we were definitely the fun ones in the group.

There was a slight halt in the food parade between the *antipasto* and *primo piatto* so that people could step outside to smoke. I really hate cigarette smoke, but in that moment I was grateful to be living in a country where it was considered normal to take a break to do so. I used the respite to visit friends at other tables.

Sometime after the *cappelli d'alpino al tartufo* (pasta with truffles), but before the *gnocchi alla crema di scampi* (gnocchi in a creamy shrimp sauce) I was ready to cry uncle. It was then that I noticed that Marco had passed on the second pasta dish.

We can do that? I looked around the table, no one else had refused anything.

I nudged him. "*Non dobbiamo mangiare tutto?*" We don't have to eat everything?

"No. You can just take the plates you want."

Now you tell me!

I didn't feel right about refusing any of the dishes — seemed ungrateful at best and rude at worst — but I did feel better about taking a few bites and then bucking up for the next. It seemed a good compromise.

As we dined, a female singer and a little band serenaded us with Italian love ballads and a couple of American wedding classics like YMCA. A few ladies got up and danced after one of the smoking breaks, but it didn't seem to be an integral part of the festivities.

And was it any wonder? I'd hardly be able to walk let alone dance after all we'd consumed.

By the time we'd stuffed in the final mouthfuls of veal and were invited to join the newlyweds back in the solarium for the cutting of the cake and the dessert buffet, I was done. A coffee bar had been set up where we'd had champagne earlier and people started in on the grappa and cognac. The whole room had become a scene out of *Willy Wonka and the Chocolate Factory* with every imaginable dessert assailing the senses. I eyed the mounds of fruits, tiramisu, éclairs, gelato, and the billowy confections of wedding cake, but I couldn't do it. Not one strawberry. Not one bite.

Stefano had ditched his tuxedo jacket but was still quite handsome in vest, shirt, and tie. Laura looked picture perfect, not a hair out of place even after three hours of eating and posing for pictures, and any mud she'd accumulated on her dress had miraculously disappeared.

Two humongous champagne flutes materialized and to cries of "*Viva gli sposi!*" the couple intertwined arms and toasted their new life together. It was a romantic, beautiful moment despite all the catcalling and shouts of "*Bacio!*" (kiss). Unexpected tears pricked at my eyes. Obviously this wedding was bringing up emotions I hadn't realized were bubbling below the surface. It was true I sometimes felt lonely on my own but I hadn't realized how much some part of me was still holding out hope for my happy ending. As much as I loved the warmth and attentiveness of the Italian men, I hadn't found many who were faithful. I had also chosen to live in a small town where most of the eligible men were spoken for, or confirmed and dedicated flirts looking for a good time. Most of the time I could find the humor in this. But then there were days when you found yourself at a wedding and it forced you to contemplate your future. I re-surveyed the dessert table. Maybe I needed some cake after all.

We sipped *spumante* and hung around for another hour before collecting our favors, which were delicate crocheted flowers created by Stefano's grandmother, the stem of each holding a dainty sachet of five Jordan almonds. The number five represents good wishes for health, wealth, fertility, longevity, and happiness for the bride and groom, and in every favor of almonds I have opened in Italy, five is the magic number.

Fabio looked at the enormous pile of crocheted handiwork and mused, "She must have started making these when Stefano was in high school. *Che lavoro!*" So much work.

We piled back into the car and I felt my eyes lids getting heavy as the road lulled me into a contented state. In the backseat, Marco and Mattia recapped the highlights of the lunch. My first Italian wedding had undeniably been an experience. Six hours from start to finish and I wouldn't need to eat for a week.

Marco, the most critical foodie of the group, gave his summation of the lunch: *"Non abbiamo mangiato ne bene ne male."* We didn't eat badly or well.

Really?

To me, the meal had been fabulous. Definitely too much, but fabulous. I guess I'd have to wait for the next wedding to have something to compare it to. I'd certainly learned one lesson: be wary of the allure of the aperitivo!

how the barriques/barrels were toasted like a crème brûlée and Francesco unquestioningly repeated it during his practice presentation at dinner with his family. Maria Stella had seemed a bit bored as Francesco spoke, but Anna and Federico hung on every word, concentration etched into their faces as they struggled to follow along in English. Nailed it, I'd thought happily when he finished, taking a celebratory sip of my Rosso di Montepulciano, before glancing at Federico who appeared to be choking on his *osso buco*.

"*Cosa ha detto?*" he demanded. What did he say? "Barrels toasted like crème brûlée?"

Being the sharp woman that I am, I quickly deduced that I'd somehow relayed erroneous information to Francesco. Anna looked everywhere but at me, while Maria Stella intently studied her pureed potatoes. No help from that quarter.

"Erm, it's my fault," I said, face flaming. I wished, not for the first time, for the superpower of teleportation. "Someone told me that when they explained the toasting of the French oak."

I was tempted to throw Fabio under the bus because I was pretty sure it was he who had relayed this incorrect tidbit, but instead I sat there and listened to Federico's fifteen-minute dissertation on how barrels are actually toasted. So for those of you who took my tour the first year I worked at Poliziano please note: crème brûlée is a scrumptious dessert with a lovely toasted crackled sugar topping but it has nothing to do with toasting wine barrels. Instead, the barrels are placed over a small fire while the staves are still open, resulting in those lovely tertiary aromas coming into our wine.

"At least your dad laughed about it afterwards," I said now to Francesco. "If he'd given me the scary raised eyebrow I would have been worried." I tried to imitate Federico's menacing arched glare and Francesco dissolved into fits of laughter.

"I think he was really laughing because your Italian was so bad back then." Francesco grinned.

"True, but it's pretty good now and he still acts like he doesn't understand me."

"*Cosa ha detto?*" we said in unison, laughing.

As it turned out, Francesco needn't have worried about his English or doing a refresher on winery processes. He was a natural with the clients. They were tickled that the son of the family was presenting the wine and he always spoke passionately about his grandfather and father's love of the territory. He usually didn't give the right information on the vintages and sometimes made stuff up, but nobody seemed to care so we just let him have fun and work on his English and his confidence. And honestly, Fabio and I were grateful to have another set of hands to help wash glasses, load cartons of wine into cars, and help us prepare for the annual Poliziano dinner, which fell during the busiest time of year.

✦　✦　✦

Before long, it was all hands on deck. The annual Poliziano "Experience" event always seemed like a good idea, a way to give back to clients and promote the winery, but the fact that it happened during the season meant trying to organize a party while still doing tastings, taking guests on tours, and the million other things we needed to get done during the day. The event had gone through many permutations over the years, first a cocktail event, then buffet lunch, and this year a catered dinner for 150 with live music and even a glass blower from Venice. They had also hired some exotic looking hostesses, whose tight white blouses and black micro-miniskirts revealed a lot of their assets, causing the men to act sillier than usual.

Thanks to the overabundant machismo of my colleagues, I'd been spared the worst of the party prep because they didn't think women could handle the heavy lifting. So I'd arrived, already gussied up, a couple of hours before the event. The brick terrace above our barrel cellar had been transformed with tents and tables and even a little stage for the band. I was tasked with creating seating cards and placing them on tables, which had been elegantly dressed in white linen. Maria Stella and Francesco helped me for about five minutes then wandered off to do something more interesting.

"Ciao, Americana!"

I set the last place cards on the table, measuring by eye the distance from each plate to the three-liter facsimile of Asinone; wine bottles were serving as centerpieces owing to Federico's abhorrence of flowers. I looked around, smiled and waved to Massimiliano who was striding toward me.

I'd met Massimiliano even before I moved to Italy. I had been staying at my friend Laura's agriturismo helping her with wedding preparations. Laura was one of the first friends I'd made in Italy and I always looked forward to staying at her place. One evening she'd hosted a pre-wedding dinner for those involved in the preparation for her big day. Massimiliano and his family, who were catering the wedding, were among the invitees.

Our first meeting had been terrible and awkward, mostly due to my lack of Italian and his insistence on teasing me the entire evening. I spent half the night in the kitchen, hiding behind the figurative skirts of Laura's mom, Marisa, so as to avoid his good-natured but relentless ribbing. I vowed that some day when my Italian was better, I would be able to put him in his place.

He was grinning now that same mischievous grin that made him decidedly boyish and had tormented me those many years ago. He was a big man, tall, robust, and paunchy, the latter no doubt a result of spending too much time sampling the food coming out of the kitchen. When we'd first met again a couple of years ago during plans for our first Poliziano event, I'd recognized him right away but wasn't sure that he remembered me. Then his eyes lit up.

"Americana, he'd said incredulously. *"Che ci fai qui?"* What are you doing here?

"I work here," I'd told him. "I live in Montepulciano." He sat down next to my computer and continued to drill me with questions, which thankfully I had been able to answer. My Italian may not have been perfect but compared to our first encounter it was brilliant.

Since that time, we always chatted when he stopped in to the winery to pick up wine for his clients or to go over menus with Fabio. And happily when he teased me, I was able to banter right back.

"What do you think of the setup?" he asked me now, proudly surveying the entire terrace on which his crew had been working nonstop for two days. The sun was lowering in the sky and the evening promised to be temperate with a warm breeze. The elegant tables, under cover of two billowy tents adorned with white lights, completed the tableau, making the setting seem rather magical.

"*Bella*," I told him. And it was.

"*Sì*, beautiful . . . like you," he told me, looking me up and down.

"*Basta*," Enough, I told him, unable to stifle a smile.

I slowly backed away and waggled my finger at him, unwilling to be drawn into a flirtation. I still marveled at how effortlessly Italians could change speeds. I loved chatting with Massimiliano and there was definitely a frisson of something between us, but he'd just broken up with his long-time girlfriend so friendship seemed the wisest course in the moment. I could hear him chuckling as I hustled away to find Fabio to see what else needed to be done.

As people started trickling in, I positioned myself in the tasting room to offer a glass of chilled chardonnay to guests who were gathering to take a tour of the winery.

Federico and Anna came over to me, escorting a tall man I didn't recognize.

I poured wine for them while Federico introduced me.

"This is Jennifer. She is American. She is a writer." This is how he always introduced me.

The man extended his hand to me. "Criswell, *giusto*?" right?

"*Sì*." He knew me, but I was sure I'd never met him. Awkward. I looked to Anna and Federico for help.

"I'm the mayor," he explained, seeing my look of confusion. "I signed all of your many, many citizenship documents." He smiled. Ahhh.

"Well, thank you very much," I said beaming, now in my mind's eye seeing his name stamped on everything in my file over the past three years, both the rejections and the final acceptance. "It was quite an involved process."

"I am just glad we got it done in the end," he said.

"Me, too. *Grazie di tutto*." Thank you for everything.

CHAPTER NINE

IL BRAVIO (BATTLE OF THE BARRELS)

The heat of August radiated off the cobblestones even in the early evening as I made my way up the *corso*. Fragrant barbecue smoke from the contrada grills spiced the air with the promise of roasting pork shanks and sausages, causing me to pick up the pace. Bravio week: my favorite week of the year. Competition, barbecues, and tradition. It was a week where you felt connected. Acquaintances would nod approvingly when they saw you wearing your district's colors. You were conscious that it may have been dumb luck that put you in a certain neighborhood but whether you were born into it or were a transplant like me, during Bravio week you belonged. The town swelled with visitors adding to the festive atmosphere. Stores stayed open late and there was definite bustle even in the wee hours. Siena may have its famous horse race, the Palio, but Montepulciano's Bravio delle Botte garners just as much enthusiasm . . . on a *slightly* smaller scale.

My contrada, Gracciano, is right past Franca's fruit and vegetable shop. Franca waved to me from inside the beaded curtain of her doorway. More than a source of locally grown fruits and vegetables, Franca shared my love of cooking with fresh ingredients and she always went out of her way to order me hard to find items like sweet potatoes, or even limes when I needed a margarita fix. She was also my go-to fruit person while Salvatore was away in Sicily. She often offered up great recipe suggestions when I eyed some unfamiliar variety of greens or tubers. I repaid her extra kindnesses in the only way I knew how—with baked goods. She was particularly fond of my banana bread.

"Ciao, Franca," I called as I passed tantalizing displays of dark red cherries and juicy apricots lounging seductively outside the shop.

I hurried past the entrance of my contrada, trying to avoid making eye contact with the Gracciano elders. Despite proudly wearing our distinctive black and green colors on my scarf complete with lion motif, tonight I was dining at a different contrada, Talosa, at the top of the town.

We have eight contrada districts in Montepulciano. Historically the districts of the town had a military role. During the warring between Siena and Florence in the 15th century Montepulciano was coveted for its bustling economy and strategic positioning between the Orcia and Chiana rivers.

These neighborhoods were also historically responsible for protecting and maintaining their section of the town's walls, defense of its gates, and even organization of the fire brigade. The pride one has for its contrada is something akin to the fervor that people feel for their hometown sports team, only deeper. It's the passion of a close-knit community that comes together to celebrate and pay homage to the history and traditions of the town. And there is, of course, the requisite friendly rivalry between the various districts. History oozes from the pores of Montepulciano every day, but during this time of year it is a pulsating and compelling entity felt not only by the inhabitants but by everyone who passes through its medieval gates.

The tradition of the Bravio is one that has been around since the 14th century. The contrada season opens with the parade on the first of May and continues through the race on the last Sunday of August with closing ceremonies in September.

Like in Siena, the Bravio in Montepulciano was originally a horse race with origins dating back to 1373. It must have been spectacular to witness decorated horses and riders charging up the *corso*, but if you have had the pleasure of walking the steep, narrow, and sometimes treacherous streets of this town, you will understand why, for issues of public safety and to avoid the townsfolk being crushed beneath horse hooves, the race was re-imagined into the barrel race of today, the *Bravio delle Botte.* A prosaic barrel race on its face, in reality it is an extreme test of skill and stamina. Each contrada has two *spingitori* (two really fit guys) who push (*spingono*) a 200-pound wine barrel from the bottom of Montepulciano over 1800 meters to the Cathedral in Piazza Grande at the top of the town. To the winning contrada goes the *"bravio"* which is a cloth panel dedicated to the town's patron saint, San Giovanni Decollato. Of course, there are also money and bragging rights at stake. But as fun as the actual race is, the festivities leading up to it are what everyone remembers.

By the time I reached Piazza Grande, I was breathing hard and decidedly *sudata.* That's Italian for sweaty, but to my ear sounds a tad more delicate. I thought of the guys who would be pushing those heavy, unwieldy barrels up the hill at breakneck speed in just a few days. *Sudatissimi.* Super sweaty!

I had to walk the periphery of the piazza because huge bleachers had been set up in the middle in preparation for festivities later that night. The Thursday night before race day is the *Corteo dei Cere,* candlelight procession. Much like the May parade, there are flag throwers, drummers, and the royal court of each *contrada* in medieval dress, but this time, as the processional winds its way through the town's districts, it is by candlelight. All the lights are turned off during the parade and for a moment you are transported back in time. Then inevitably a young drummer or flag thrower tugs at his velvet tunic because he is dying in the heat, or one of the bystanders steps on a flaming candle, and you are brought back to reality.

Talosa is one of the town's oldest contrade with roots back to the 11th century. The terrace of the Palazzo Ricci is home to its dinners during Bravio week. I entered the courtyard of the palazzo where Talosa's red and yellow flag was flying and scanned for my British friends Gill and Adrian. Before I spotted them, I saw their daughter Tamara waiting tables, her long blonde hair skimmed back in a tight ponytail, a Talosa scarf neatly tied around her neck as she made her way through long picnic tables of hungry diners jammed elbow to elbow. Tamara somehow managed to make the Talosa colors look good.

Esthetically Talosa is my least favorite color scheme, as every time I see the flag throwers in their bright yellow and red tunics and tights, I am reminded of Ronald McDonald. It's the only *contrada* that looks as if it went cheap and cheerful and got a really good deal on closeout yellow fabric that no one else wanted.

Colors aside, the dinners at Talosa were good. A friendly rivalry existed between each district that went beyond the race. The cooks in each *contrada* had developed specialties that prompted long lines of hungry and eager diners each summer. As soon as the Bravio calendar of events was published, Janet and I would eagerly peruse the menus. We were always happy to feast on the *nana* (duck) in porchetta of Collazzi. And I was a big fan of the *stinco*, (pork shank) that Poggiolo did so well. Winning recipes were included in the official Contrada cookbook. Marinella's *pici* and sugo Toscano had won some years back.

The line was long and the smell heavenly as the grill masters fired up Florentine steaks and pork loin. Talosa was also one of the few contrade that served meals with real plates and glasses.

I was late leaving work, so I'd texted Gill to order for me. I'd barely said hello and slung my leg over the table's bench when heaping plates of food arrived. Mine was pork loin with roasted apples. Gill filled my glass with wine, while I glanced around the terrace. The place was already packed, voices raised accordingly to be heard above the din. Marinella's son Giacomo caught my eye and he waved to me. I smiled and raised my glass in salute. Tightness eased from my shoulders. I soaked in the feeling of comfort that came with no longer being the new girl.

"We started drinking without you," Gill said pointing to a bottle of Vino Nobile. "They didn't have Poliziano. Hope this is okay."

"I can drink Poliziano any time." I inspected the Boscarelli label. One of my favorite cantinas. I sipped happily and shared a couple of stories about my day including the reason I was late.

"So the last tasting of the day was with one of our French clients. Fabio always does the tastings for Jean-Jacques because he speaks a little French. Jean-Jacques is a well-known orthodontist in France. As I'm cleaning tables, I hear

Fabio switch into Italian and begin telling Jean-Jacques about some problem with his son Pietro's teeth. Then Fabio calls to me to ask if I can finish the tasting because he has to make a phone call.

I asked what was going on, but Fabio didn't answer so I continued the tasting for Jean-Jacques in Italian. Five minutes later Fabio comes back in with his wife Erika and their son Pietro in tow.

Before I can wrap my head around what is happening, Fabio opens Pietro's mouth and begins showing the orthodontist his son's teeth like he is some sort of show pony. And Jean-Jacques is totally cool with it. This man is on vacation in Tuscany and he gets up from his wine tasting and begins to do an exam.

I keep staring at the scene in incredulity and tell Fabio I couldn't believe he had just done that.

Fabio just shrugs as if this is all perfectly normal, and asks, 'Where is the problem?'"

After pausing to take a sip of my wine I added, "I left before the diagnosis, but I hope he at least gave that orthodontist a bottle of wine."

Adrian and Gill laughed, knowing Fabio all too well.

"But what about you guys? How are the guests this year?" I asked Adrian. Adrian and Gill had bought a gorgeous piece of land from two brothers who owned a sheep farm, and the sheep still roamed the fields, slowly grazing from one end to another, keeping them nicely trimmed.

Gill always got upset when the sheep had their babies in the spring and the lambs were taken away. "I just tell myself they're going on holiday," she'd told me. "Otherwise it's just too horrible."

That being said, I'd spent Easter with them last year and we'd dined on a leg of lamb that one of the farmers had given them. Mint jelly, anyone?

The property boasted over a hundred ancient olive trees badly in need of pruning; this I knew intimately because I'd helped harvest them two years running. They had renovated a decrepit farmhouse and turned it into a beautiful villa for guests as well as a smaller apartment for them and their three girls. Adrian had done most of the work himself. He handled the hospitality while Gill did the cleaning changeover and tried to avoid interaction with their guests.

"The Americans are the worst as always," Adrian teased. "They leave the lights on and the A/C going even when they aren't at home."

Gill and I exchanged glances and smiled as we settled in to listen to the latest edition of "nightmare guests." Adrian didn't disappoint. He munched steadily on grilled sausages all the while regaling us with stories of broken toilet seats, duvets stained with red wine, bottles floating in the pool, and strip poker shenanigans on the patio.

Tamara came over, bringing us some extra baskets of steaming fries -perks of having your daughter work at the *contrada*. "Tell her about when Dominique found the handcuffs on the gazebo."

We all laughed because the Belgian sex-game couple had been the winning story from last year.

"I am sure they were just using them to hang their towels, dear." Gill said.

"Yes, because I always bring my handcuffs on vacation to Tuscany in case there aren't enough clothes pegs," Adrian snorted.

The evening passed too quickly and as Adrian and Gill headed to the square to wait for the festivities, I made my way down the hill in time to watch the parade with my contrada.

✦   ✦   ✦

Fortune smiled on Gracciano as Sunday's Bravio resulted in a win for "us". When the starter gun went off and the sirens signaled the start of the race, I'd cheered loudly for Piero, one of our *spingitore* as the barrels came storming up the corso. Piero worked in the vineyards at Poliziano, and he trained all year long for the race. His thighs looked like tree trunks from running up the steep hills and he was always recognizable from his blond ponytail flapping behind him. The race itself was over in about seven minutes; the celebrating, however, went on much longer. And this year, after two evenings of merry-making, I somehow found myself committed to helping out at the victory dinner. Damn you, never-ending bottles of Vino Nobile.

When I'd first moved to town, I had tried to participate in my contrada, hoping to help out in the kitchen during Bravio week with the preparation of the dinners like the one I'd just attended at Talosa. Marinella was one of the main cooks for Gracciano and since I didn't have much work in those first lean years, I often offered up my time and help with a newcomer's enthusiasm. They were always politely declined. I put it down to being a *straniera* (foreigner), but it was disheartening even with Marinella trying to soften the blow. "*Lascia perdere. Meglio se non ti confondi con noi.*" Let it go. It's better if you don't get mixed up with us.

That being said, she always headed up to the Gracciano kitchen, apron in hand, not looking at all unhappy about going.

That is until this summer.

Marinella's latest scans showed that the cancer had returned and this time she struggled to maintain a positive outlook. She didn't talk much about it, but sometimes she'd make comments about not being around in the future. My usual reaction was anger and denial. A world without Marinella was clearly unthinkable.

"They asked me to work the Victory Dinner," I had told her one morning as I set out on my walk with Cinder. My old girl spent so much time at Marinella's in the summer that she always pulled me toward the gate if she heard Marinella's voice in the garden. "Are you going to be there?" Marinella hadn't been active in the contrada much this summer, but I was hopeful nonetheless.

She shook her head. "I don't have the energy to be in the kitchen for hours on end. I am making the ragù and I will drop that off, but you will be fine with the other ladies."

I was disappointed but I understood. Any excitement I'd felt at finally being included was definitely tempered.

I reported for duty on the evening of the dinner with more than a few butterflies. I had been told only to wear a white shirt, so I figured I would be serving, but I had no idea what else was going to be expected of me.

One of the people who always participated in the organization of our *contrada* was Robert, an American whom I had met in my first months living in Montepulciano. He was the one who had referred me to Anna and Federico to teach English to the kids. How an American got the job of heading the *contrada* dinners, I never was quite sure. But as it's a thankless job by all accounts and Robert was an easygoing and organized guy, I am sure this played into it. Unfortunately for me, Robert wasn't at this dinner.

I sidled up to some other white-shirted folk. Two of them were dressed like me in white tees and jeans and three obviously had done the cater-waiter thing before and were sporting the ubiquitous black pants and white button downs detested by waitstaff the world over. Who among us hasn't done time in that world of stifling but easy to clean polyester?

One of the professional white shirts introduced herself as Patrizia and told me this was her first time working in Gracciano but she'd helped out in some of the other *contrade* in the past.

Patrizia led me over to a bald guy holding a clipboard. I think I heard someone call him Meme.

"Thanks for coming," he said. "Tonight's dinner is a little different from the regular meals. There is a fixed menu and so instead of people ordering, we will be bringing around platters and serving everyone individually. You two go see if you can help organize in the kitchen. There is a mountain of prosciutto to slice."

While some of the *contrade* have lovely gardens for their events, the dinners at Gracciano were held in the parking area of Sant'Agostino church. Long tables and benches were already in place, and they'd been set with silverware and glasses for wine. A few potted plants had been peppered about to try and distract from the fact that we were dining in a parking lot. The air wasn't as stifling as the weeks before, but it was still quite warm for September. I hoped we'd get a breeze while we were working. The one thing you could usually count on in Montepulciano was a drop in temperature and a *venticino* after sundown.

I had never been in the kitchen or the recreation room, so Patrizia and I walked around and got familiar with the setup. Outside the kitchen, two large grills were firing, the delectable aroma of woodchips and grilled meat making my stomach growl in its usual Pavlovian response to a barbecue.

A small room off to the side of the kitchen had become the staging area for platters of crostini laden with toppings like pâté, pecorino and pear, and what looked to be some type of mushroom spread. There was also a whole table dedicated to bread that had already been sliced and arranged in baskets. I may not be the biggest fan of the unsalted Tuscan bread, but when it comes to antipasto, I'd seen my friends polish off basket after basket with their salty *salumi*. We served so much prosciutto during the season at Poliziano that I could barely look at it in the winter. One of our clients, Lisa, a pretty, freckled redhead from Seattle, had summed it up perfectly, making me burst out laughing as she dove into a platter of prosciutto that Fabio had prepared for her group, proudly declaring, "I've eaten so much cured meat on this trip that I can't see my feet." Truth!

There was no one in the kitchen when we arrived, so we took the initiative and began preparing the cold cuts. Being somewhat of an expert with the slicer after a few seasons at Poliziano, I sliced and Patrizia laid the thin pieces of salami, *capocollo*, and prosciutto on platters and covered them with plastic wrap.

We were about a half hour into our work when my neighbor Pia came in. Barely five feet tall, Pia had the outward appearance of a kindly aunt. So, no one was more surprised than me when she surveyed the kitchen with a scowl, evidently checking to see if we had disturbed anything.

She then began shouting at us. "*Fuori!*" Out!

Patrizia calmly explained that we'd been asked to prepare the cold cuts, but Pia's stony glare brooked no opposition. "Get. Out. Of. My kitchen," she bellowed again. For a tiny woman, she had quite the set of lungs.

Patrizia and I beat a hasty retreat. My face was flaming and I was almost in tears, but Patrizia just laughed.

"So this is Gracciano," she said. "I've heard that the women in the kitchen were quite territorial, but this is a little extreme." I opened my mouth to defend Marinella, but then closed it again. I had never actually seen her in action in the *contrada* so maybe she went into crazy mode like Pia. Could this be why she had tried to dissuade me from helping in the past?

"Let's go find something else to do," I said.

In the end, after a brief explanation to clipboard guy, we opened bottles of Rosso di Montepulciano and Vino Nobile and some type of chardonnay, and then placed a few bottles of red and white on each table.

When it was time to serve the dinner, I really didn't want to go back in the kitchen, but there was no other choice. Our little squad of 6 was about to serve 120 people.

The antipasto went fine. We'd plated the crostini and added slices of the *salumi*, so we just had to put the plates on trays and walk around giving a plate to each person. I knew lots of people so it was enjoyable greeting everyone as I set down their plates.

The trouble came when it was time for the pasta.

Pia and her cohorts had prepared huge pans of cannelloni, which were ridiculously heavy. This was to be followed by homemade *pici* pasta with Marinella's ragù. I wasn't about to back down from the obvious challenge thrust at us, but by the time I had raced back to the kitchen for my third tray, my arm muscles were quivering as I attempted to hold the pan in one arm and serve with the other. Piero and his winning squad were in my section and those guys ate second and third helpings of everything. This was partly due to the fact that Marinella's ragù was always a favorite; I'd hoped there'd be a little of the *pici* left for us when we finished, but as I served up another pan, it didn't seem likely. I concentrated on willing my arm not to give out so the fragrant saucy strands wouldn't end up on anyone's lap. I wasn't quite flinging pasta at diners by the end, but I was relieved when we moved on to the roasted meats.

Until I saw the platter of lamb hit the deck. A white-haired man, whom I knew to be Pia's husband, was filling a platter with grilled lamb when the platter buckled and it all crashed to the ground.

We all took a deer-in-the-headlights beat and then the swearing started.

Patrizia moved to block the entrance to the kitchen so that Pia and the other ladies couldn't see what had happened.

"Five-second rule," I called wanting to save the poor man from Pia's wrath. We hurriedly began picking up the pieces, dusting them off and throwing them back on the grill. It was quite gross but I had worked in enough restaurants in my youth to know that this was how it was done. But I'll admit that when it was time to serve the roasted meats, I tried to steer everyone toward the chicken.

At the end of the meal, spumante was offered, followed by a toast to our winning spingitori and trainers. As I refilled his glass, Piero thanked me for helping out and said he'd see me at work. I smiled happily, enjoying the warm sensation of belonging. It was almost midnight by the time they began cutting the huge sheet cake, and I was exhausted. And disgusting. The servers in their permanent press still looked fine, but our t-shirted contingent looked pretty bad. I had some lovely Jackson Pollock type splashes of sauce on mine thanks to an errant strand of *pici* that had jumped its pan, and from having had to balance some of the heaviest trays on my boobs.

Our little band munched on cake and drank a bottle of bubbly as we congratulated each other on, in the end, a job well done. Even as we exchanged numbers and joked about seeing each other the next summer, I was already compiling a list of excuses that I vowed to have ready for the future. For me the contrada experience was going into the same annals as grape harvesting. I came. I saw. I never wanted to do it again.

Il Sugo di Marinella

- 2 chicken livers (already cooked)
- 900 g. ground beef
- 100 g. ground pork
(1 kilo = 2 1/2 pounds)
- 2 carrots
- 2 yellow onions
- handful of parsley
- salt and pepper
- 1 c. olive oil
- 2 1/2 cans of 800 g whole peeled tomatoes (use hand mixer to make passato)
- 1 glass of red wine

Chop chicken livers. Chop carrot, onion and parsley by hand or in food processor. In a low pot, mix by hand the meat, vegetables, oil and salt and pepper. Begin browning over high heat. Marinella always said, "*Il segreto dell fare il sugo è la rosalatura.*" The secret to making a ragu is the browning. The browning process will take a long time, around 40 minutes. You will see the color change to a deep caramel brown. This step is so important because otherwise you'll just have boiled meat.

After the meat is browned, add the red wine. Cook for 5 minutes or until the alcohol has evaporated. Add tomatoes, bring to a boil and then lower flame. Cover and cook 3-4 hours, stirring occasionally. You'll know its ready when the oil comes back to the surface. Adjust seasoning.

AUTUNNO /
AUTUMN

CHAPTER TEN

COMFORT FOOD

Autumn in Tuscany is a spectacular dance of color. In September, deep purple bunches of grapes seduce the senses during harvest as they overflow buckets and tractors on their journey into wine. Then the hues of the sloping hillsides change as temperatures start to dip. Yellow foliage from Sangiovese vineyards mingles with the orangey-red tones of the cabernet and merlot, a shimmering palette on nature's canvas.

As much as I loved these crisp autumn days, and the accompanying aroma of woodsmoke pluming out of chimneys, it was also a chill reminder that winter loomed ahead. And with it, months and months without a regular paycheck. Cinder had probably gotten used to my quoting Ruth Hussey's line from *The Philadelphia Story*, "Belts will be worn a little tighter this year." My pronouncements were met with Cinder's signature regal head tilt as if to say, "If anyone is going to miss a meal this year, it had better not be me."

Each winter had gotten a little easier, a little less lean, but I still felt a pit in my stomach thinking of trying to get through. I knew there would be English lessons with some of the local kids, but history had taught me that students were not the most reliable source of income.

One of the things that made winter a little more bearable was my friendship with Janet and Ken. Invites for Sunday lunches were frequent, and it was always a relaxing way to spend an afternoon. Both of them cooked, Ken usually did the pasta course and Janet had a repertoire of roasts and comfort food. They had had me over a few days earlier for a hot meal in an even hotter house. Ken liked to keep things toasty and it had been hovering around 80 degrees.

After shepherd's pie, a bottle of Vino Nobile, and two glasses of vin santo, I was melty and ready to sleep. I listened as Ken recounted one of his stories from his years in the Navy, willing my eyes not to close. Reading my thoughts Ken went over to the stereo and put on some lively music.

I was too stuffed for dessert, so Janet packed up some apple strudel for me to take home. "We leave in a few days, so I will drop off some other bits and bobs from the fridge for you before we go." Janet and Ken were off to France for a couple of weeks. Ken was a prolific painter. He'd recently begun doing some still lifes, but most of his work took its inspiration from the Tuscan countryside. His style leaned toward impressionism, so he was eager to see the birthplace of Paul Cézanne in Aix-en-Provence, and then he and Janet planned to tour around the French countryside.

"What will you do with yourself next week, possum?" Janet asked as she packed up some shepherd's pie for me as well.

"Olive harvesting. Charles and Peter said they needed some help. They have a massive number of trees to harvest. Other than that, maybe a cooking lesson with Marinella."

"How is she doing?" Janet asked as she placed the containers in a bag.

"It's hard to know. She won't talk about it. She doesn't seem to be in any pain, but she tires easily."

"Give her my best," Janet said as we parted.

When I got home, I grabbed Cinder and we went for a quick walk around the parking area. I glanced toward Janet and Ken's window and could see them in the lounge, locked in an embrace, dancing. It was a sweet scene and one, no doubt, that Ken could have captured beautifully in a painting.

✦   ✦   ✦

A few days later I was back in the warmth of Marinella's kitchen, separating the ribs from *cavolo nero* (Tuscan kale) then rough chopping both the kale and a piece of *cavolo verza* (savoy cabbage) for *ribollita*, my favorite Tuscan soup. And one I would make often over the course of the winter. There were lots of variations of this famous vegetable soup, whose name means reboiled. It was a traditional *minestra* that families could reboil and eat off of for a few days, hence *ribollita*. After cooking, it was customary to layer the soup with thin slices of stale Tuscan bread, letting the soup soften the bread for a few hours and creating a delicious union that is then reheated before serving. Both Fabio and Marinella reheated their *ribollita* in the oven instead of on the stove and I did this as well, liking the little bit of crust that formed on the top. I had tried most of the *ribollita* offered in the restaurants of Montepulciano and my favorites were always those that had a little less bread and a little more broth. A drizzle of olive oil on top just before serving was pure heaven.

Marinella manned the stove, sauteing chopped onions in her big soup pot, before adding some peeled tomatoes. She then prepared the white beans she had soaked the night before and had cooked this morning. She ran half of them through a food mill, creating a cannellini cream, which she added back to the cooking water and remaining whole beans. I diced carrots and potatoes.

Marinella looked well, but while I could detect no outward signs of illness, I knew better than to ask how she was feeling.

"Now that the season is winding down, maybe we can do some walks in the countryside?" I asked her in Italian.

"*Si, forse.*" Her eyes twinkled. "*Le tue abilità di raccolta dei funghi potrebbero essere migliorate.*" Your mushroom foraging skills could use improvement.

I laughed. "*É vero.*" True. I had my doubts if I would ever become proficient in that department.

We piled the cabbage into the pot, then topped it with potatoes and carrots. We stirred it down a few times as we chatted. The aromatic steam wafting from the pot added to the coziness of the room.

"*Domani, se non piove, iniziamo con gli olivi,*" Marinella said. If it doesn't rain, we will start harvesting olives tomorrow. "*Anche tu, no? Vai dagli amici?*" You too, right. With your friends?

"*Sì, non vedo l'ora.*" I can't wait. Marinella put her hand on my forehead like she was checking for a fever. Harvesting olives was work after all. But to me, it was also enjoyable.

I chuckled. "*Dai, si diverte.*" Come on, it's fun.

"Sì sì." Oh yes.

After the vegetables had reduced down, we added the beans and cooking water and let everything simmer together for another half hour. While we waited, we made plans to go to the market on Thursday.

After adjusting the seasoning, Marinella sliced stale Tuscan bread and we layered some of the soup over the bread in a big terracotta pot. Then Marinella repeated the layering in the smaller earthenware dish that I had brought over.

As she handed me the soup, I said, "*Ora ci serve olio nuovo.*" Now we just need some new oil.

"It's coming," Marinella said. It always tickled me when she attempted a few words in English. I put my hand to her forehead like I was checking for a fever.

Her laugh followed me out the door.

CHAPTER ELEVEN

EXTRA VIRGIN CONVERSION

My olive oil obsession dates back to my first stay at Laura's agriturismo more than seven years before. On vacation with my best friend Cheryl, we'd stumbled upon Laura's farm La Bruciata, just a couple of kilometers outside of Montepulciano. We'd arrived at the end of November, the cold air smelled as if it might snow at any moment. The olive harvest had just finished.

In our apartment Laura had left a welcome basket with coffee, homemade jams, eggs, and a small, unlabeled bottle of olive oil. After a day of sightseeing, we'd built a fire and unpacked the bread, wine, salami, and cheese that we'd decided would be dinner. We uncorked the little bottle, liberally dousing pieces of bread in vibrant green oil.

And then we tasted it.

The world stopped for a second. I didn't quite hear angels singing, but close. The olive oil was a revelation: a bright grassy aroma, then fruity and peppery on the palate, making my mouth want to shout with happiness. I had never tasted anything like it. By day two we'd finished the bottle. So we'd asked for more. By the end of the trip, I was enamored; I bought as many bottles as I could stuff into my suitcase.

And that was just the beginning.

The following year when I went back with my friend Will, I shipped home five liters. Laura was incredulous. She and her mom, Marisa conferred, debating whether or not to inquire.

"What are you going to do with all this oil?" Laura asked as she pasted her label on the big green tin, then swaddled it in bubble wrap.

"She's going to bathe in it," Will told her. "She finds that it keeps the skin supple."

Laura laughed heartily, but I could see her mulling that over.

The problem only got worse once I moved here. So in order to feed my addiction, I began helping friends with their harvesting.

Unlike grape harvesting, which is tough on the back and requires periodic doses of Advil, olive harvesting is quite satisfying with an almost Zen-like peacefulness. There isn't much to it. The part that takes the longest is getting the nets untangled and spread out under the trees, and waiting until the dew is off the fruit, so it is dry as you begin harvesting. Then you simply run your hands down the branches and little green and purple olives begin dancing their way down to the net.

Having already helped Gill and Adrian a couple of times, this year I said yes to another set of British friends, Charles and Peter, when they had mentioned they'd needed some help. They were relatively new arrivals to Montepulciano and had taken an old stone farmhouse and transformed it into a bed and breakfast that was a showstopper. The property was considerable with acres and acres of almond, apricot, and fig trees, a vineyard, and more than 2,000 olive trees. Harvesting would take a few weeks.

On day one, I gave Cinder a kiss and tucked my old girl under her favorite blanket. Cinder loved olive harvesting, but unfortunately she delighted in hunting for and eating sheep and deer poop, then inevitably after that workout she felt it necessary to stretch out on the nets on top of all of the olives, rolling on her back and using them as a personal massager. So this year she was tasked with holding down the fort.

Charles and Peter picked me up early, and with their two basset hounds, Harold and Maude, at our sides, we began trekking across wet grasses of a rolling terrain with spectacular views of the entire valley. The day was gray and cold as November was wont to be and the mesh of my old trusty Asics (which had received a reprieve from the donation bin after being converted into olive harvesting shoes) became damp as we neared the first tree. The property was once a part of La Foce, the grand estate owned by Iris Origo and her husband, famous for shielding Italians from the Nazis during World War II. Iris herself had shepherded local children to safety in Montepulciano. On my first visit, the boys had showed me caves where soldiers had taken refuge from the fighting.

Peter had already spread a net under an ancient tree whose trunk had the approximate circumference of a Fiat 500. Gill and Adrian had one such mammoth tree on their property as well that we'd nicknamed "home tree." This must be his cousin. The big trees were always the most satisfying to harvest because with their yield you could usually fill at least one and sometimes two crates.

We circled the tree twice, making sure we hadn't missed any olives, which sometimes were hidden in the silvery foliage until the light shifted, then gathered the net and carefully funneled the olives into the crates. The morning passed swiftly and we peeled off hoodies and vests as the sun began to peek through the clouds. Peter and I went tree to tree harvesting by hand, while Charles used one of the electric rakes that we called the "shaky shaky" because it rattled the top of the trees and caused the olives to come off at a faster rate. They were becoming more and more popular for harvesting because you could get each tree done quite quickly, but it definitely wasn't as satisfying. And if you ask my friend Keith who is becoming quite the olive oil baron, it does some damage to the olive in the same way that machine harvesting grapevines can damage the fruit. The other problem with the shaky shaky is that you can't have a conversation when you are next to it because it is LOUD. So it renders impossible one of the best parts of olive harvesting: the camaraderie. Chatting as you work on a crisp autumn morning, the scent of wood smoke drifting on the breeze as you make your way around the trees, trying to step lightly so as not to crush the delicate orbs underfoot — this is olive harvesting as it is has always been done. Like many things in Tuscany, the traditional ways are often the best.

After a quick lunch break of ham sandwiches on Charles' homemade bread followed by my brownies (brownies should always be an integral part of the harvesting process as they provide energy and deliciousness), we moved on to a section of younger trees on a steep slope. The trees didn't have many olives so instead of putting down the nets, Charles began rummaging in the back of the SUV to find baskets.

Peter launched a fanny pack at me and I strapped it around my waist.

"Fanny packs? You can't hold many olives in a fanny —"

I stopped as both Charles and Peter hooted hysterically. Harold and Maude began to dance around excitedly.

"What's so funny? Fanny?" And as soon I said it, I began to giggle too as I remembered that "fanny" for the Brits was "vagina," not "butt" as it was for us Americans.

"You definitely shouldn't put too many olives in your fanny," Peter sputtered. They convulsed with laughter as they grabbed baskets and packs.

"Come on, boys, fannies to the ready," I called as we resumed harvesting amid much laughter. As you might imagine the rest of the afternoon was filled with lines such as "My fanny is overflowing," "Where should I unload my fanny?," "Let me just strap on my fanny," and so on.

The autumn sun was setting as we hauled the heavy crates back to the house. The uneven terrain became treacherous as we lost the light, prompting us to walk slowly. We balanced each crate carefully so as not to lose any of our bounty.

We added the day's spoils to those of the day before and, with tired satisfaction, surveyed the cellar stacked with orange and green crates brimming with olives. Charles would take them to the *frantoio* the next morning to be pressed. You needed to get the olives there within a few days of harvesting or they could become moldy. This meant working long hours because some of the pressing places required a minimum of 250 kilos before you could use their facility.

Then it was pressed and *olio nuovo* (new oil) was born.

There is something immensely satisfying in consuming a product that comes as a result of your labors on the land. Although tired from the day's exertions, covered in scratches from battling branches, and with sap-stained hands resembling a warrior's, it gave me pleasure to imagine my Italian ancestors looking down on me proudly.

Either that or they were shaking their heads bemusedly at this Tuscan tradition because according to Salvatore in Sicily his family just waits until the olives fall off the trees to harvest them!

✦　　✦　　✦

Not long after I finished harvesting with Charles and Peter, I had an opportunity to help my Cortona friends, Tania and Keith, bottle their oil. I discovered that getting that fragrant, gorgeous oil was a little more involved that I had imagined.

Tania and Keith had become great mates. They were from California and had been living here a few years longer than me. They still had a California vibe about them: Keith looked like a windswept surfer dude on the outside, always in flip-flops, but under this crunchy exterior lurked the heart and brain of a computer genius cum entrepreneur; and Tania, happiest when just home from the beach, always attired in flowing dresses, a family of delicate butterfly tattoos seeming to float on her back as if on the sea, all of this belying a quick and sometimes biting wit.

I first met Tania at Poliziano. She was doing wine tours for friends and would bring clients to us. As we got to know each other she would bring Fabio and me gifts of tomatoes, peppers, and cucumbers from her garden. One time she'd even brought me two ears of Silver Queen corn from seeds specially ordered from the States, and I almost wept.

Sharing a love of dogs, sushi, and wine, she and Keith had become a part of my intimate circle of friends here that kept me grounded. This was something that had enhanced my life in Tuscany, expanding friendships and growing my support system. These were friends with whom you could share your ups and downs over a glass of wine and come away feeling as if it was all going to be okay. We always joked that as much as we loved Italy, sometimes you just needed to bitch in your own language. I didn't see Tania and Keith often because even though Cortona was only a half hour away, without a car it was an expensive taxi ride.

The olive oil business had been Keith's dream and together with Tania's marketing and design skills, and a lot of grit and determination, they had slowly turned the dream into reality. *L'arte*, the art of the olive tree, was born.

The frigid day was spitting rain when Tania and Keith picked me up for a day of bottling at the olive press near Rusciolo. I had never been inside a frantoio before and was unprepared for how modern it was.

Where were the huge stone wheels that would crush the olives?

The large warehouse-like room was filled with fancy, state of the art machinery that would clean, extract, and deliver the exquisite oil without heating it. In other words, cold pressed. The romantic image of this process I had held had gone the way of stomping grapes by foot. Instead, moving escalators brought the cleaned olives up into the "press," which were large yellow machines using a centrifuge system to extract the oil in a clean, ecological way, and assuring that the oil doesn't become oxidized. LED display boards above each terminal told the owners how many kilos of olives were being processed and how much oil extracted. The only nod to bygone days was the huge stone fireplace in one corner where bread could be toasted and fragrant new oil sampled and shared with friends. The grassy, fruity aroma emanating from the new oil was heady.

"I've got the bread," Keith told me, pointing to the fireplace with a smile. "Liquid gold will soon be ours . . . after we're done working."

"You know me so well," I said. "I may make t-shirts for next year: Will work for oil."

Keith chuckled as we went out to unload the car.

Keith and Tania now have acres and acres of their own olive trees around Cortona, but that year their oil was produced in partnership with a local farmer. The farmer, Rinaldo, was the real deal. His family had worked the land for generations and when the landowning *contessa* (countess) who owned the property died, he had been given the opportunity to purchase it. The olive trees dated back to 800 AD.

Rinaldo didn't just do olives. He was the quintessential Tuscan farmer. He made knife handles from the bark of the olive trees, he cultivated grain, butchered his own pigs, and made his own prosciutto. He was missing a couple of fingers and that just added to his maleness.

The rain began to pour heavily as we organized supplies in the bottling room. Tania set us up at a table with a tiny bottling apparatus for the small bottles. I was in charge of applying labels as each bottle was filled and closed.

As we worked, I could hear lots of chatter from the main room. The energy there was high as farmers stood in clusters, conversing while waiting for their olives to be pressed.

I'd been concentrating on getting Tania's new pewter labels precisely centered on each bottle, so I didn't realize at first that there was trouble with the big bottling machine that was supposed to fill the liter bottles. A group of men standing around the machine kept trying to put Keith's bottles through but they didn't seem to be fitting properly. They conferred, scratching chins at this problem.

"*Tampone*," said one man, his voice high and squeaky like Mickey Mouse. *Tampone*? I looked askance at Tania and Keith who were by now starting to get a bit agitated as hundreds of bottles remained unfilled.

CRACK! The sound of breaking glass reverberated throughout the room as another bottle went into the machine and broke when the nozzle thingy went into it. Turns out the *tampone* was the nozzle, which went into the bottle and filled it to a certain level.

"The neck of your bottles isn't the right size," declared Mickey Mouse guy after another bottle cracked.

The frustration of everyone in the room was palpable. Compared to the relaxation of harvesting the olives, bottling was shaping up to be stressful.

"Your Italian is good," Tania told me. "Can you speak to the woman where we bought the bottles and explain what's happening?"

"Sure." We phoned the bottle purveyor, and I explained the problem as best I could, then passed the phone to Mickey Mouse who gave his side of the events.

The consensus seemed to be that we needed different bottles.

Fuming, Keith packed up all of the bottles and went out into the driving rain to return them to the glass factory over an hour away. The little radio in the bottling room warned of flooding on the highway.

When Keith arrived at the glass place, the woman we'd spoken to measured the neck of the bottles and declared them to be the correct size.

"*Il tampone è troppo grande,*" she told Keith. The nozzle is too big. Keith called Tania from the road with the news and made his way back to the *frantoio* with the same bottles.

Tania looked as if she was going to kill Mickey Mouse as she angrily let him know that it wasn't our problem, it was their bleeping bottling machine.

The men conferred again. The *tampone* was changed and a smaller nozzle inserted. Keith returned with the bottles and after a two-hour delay, the same bottles went into the machine, the *tampone* worked perfectly, and the bottling of the large bottles finally got underway.

The tension eased. We filled bottles, put on their tops and labels, and even managed to joke a little. We turned up the radio, the music helping to keep the energy level high for our assembly line production.

As the day wore on, I noticed fewer and fewer farmers bringing in their olives for pressing because of the weather. And by the time we finished and packed up supplies so Tania and Keith could drive me home, the A1 highway was closed because of flooding.

Sadly, there wasn't time to toast bread to sample the oil, but Tania gave me a couple of bottles to say thank you for helping. Between this and the oil I'd earned from Charles and Peter, I would have plenty for the winter. As Keith was fond of saying, "You should always have backups for your backups." I'm pretty sure he hadn't meant olive oil, nevertheless, this girl was feeling pretty darn prepared.

CHAPTER TWELVE

THE FUNERAL

We hurtled down the highway at speeds that by Italian standards were probably not unheard of but to me seemed as if the SUV would lift off the ground at any moment. The vehicle in front of us was a hearse carrying the body of Janet's husband, Ken. The hearse driver was in a hurry for reasons known only to him. Both vehicles had their headlights ablaze, but this was no sedate funeral procession of hearse followed by a parade of mourners. Instead, we could barely keep up with the deranged driver ahead of us. We shot past a police car, the officer seemingly unconcerned at the high-speed chase occurring a lane over.

Every time we hit a bump, we were sure Ken's coffin was going to come lurching out the back of the hearse and onto the road in front of us. I caught Peter's eye in the rearview mirror as he gripped the steering wheel tightly. He floored the SUV as we continued to lose ground, his dubious expression making me want to laugh. I kept it together, then looked at Janet sitting beside Peter, who looked at me and then at Peter. We let out a collective hysterical laugh.

"Ken would have appreciated the absurdity of this," Janet said.

And she was right.

Ken had had a wicked sense of humor. And perhaps it was because he was an Englishman that the whole scene seemed like something out of Monty Python skit. I kept the "But I'm not dead yet," quote to myself, but it was racing around in my brain along with the sound of coconuts clacking together.

The news of Ken's massive heart attack had taken everyone by surprise. Yes, he had been 86 and yes, he had slowed down a lot in the past year, but he and Janet had just returned from their week in Aix-en-Provence. He had returned in good spirits full of stories of their adventures.

They'd rushed him to the hospital in Siena because it was understood that while our local hospital was good, it was not the place you wanted to be for a trauma or life-threatening event. Ken held on for two weeks and then they returned him to the hospital in Montepulciano, where he passed peacefully.

I stayed with Janet as much as I could, hugging her tightly and making sure she remembered to eat. I couldn't even imagine a loss so great after 30 years of marriage. I let my own tears flow when I returned to my house. Cinder snuggled close to me, comforting me as always.

Janet hadn't let me visit Ken in the hospital during his last few days, insisting that she didn't want me to see him as the shell of his former self, barely conscious and hooked up to machines. I'd protested, but in the end respected her wishes. I held on to the happy memories I had of Ken: our conversations about writing, photography, and art, as well as those Sunday lunches where he'd shown off culinary skills honed in his bachelor days, then sipping limoncello or vin santo as we lingered at the table. Janet's house was filled with the legacy of Ken's work. His landscapes of Montepulciano and the surrounding countryside were love letters to our town. My own apartment boasted three of his paintings. Gazing at the fields of poppies, country lanes, and rustic houses, I could easily picture him sitting in the grassy fields outside of town, his whistle commingling with the birdsong overhead while his keen eye captured what so many of us wished we could. Most of us instead resorted to quick snaps on our Smartphones.

Ken's death was a stark reminder that life in Tuscany was like life anywhere. There was beauty and enormous joy. But there was also sadness. Just as each season had its birth and renewal, death was also a part of it. Every time the cold November wind swept up our street and insinuated itself under windowsills and through doorways, the chilly air seemed to accentuate our loss. Sometimes when the wind whistled I was sure I could hear Ken.

With Ken's passing, Janet and I got a lesson in Italian funerary customs. I knew from seeing the death announcements in town that almost immediately after someone died, large poster-sized notices would go up on the various message boards around town. They were a way to notify the community at large of the death of a loved one. The announcement typically had the person's name and age and sometimes the nickname that person was known by all his life. This addition was to avoid any head-scratching confusion, wondering who the heck Giovanni Umberto was. Instead, it was clarified. Giovanni Umberto *detto "Gufo."* One could surmise from this that maybe Giovanni had been wise beyond his years and so had been dubbed "owl" or, the more likely scenario, that he had worn thick glasses his whole life giving him an owlish aspect. I pictured Giovanni looking down on the proceedings, pleased with the turnout of mourners but a bit disappointed that "owl" was going to follow him into the afterlife.

The announcements also provided information about the funeral arrangements so that everyone knew which church was holding services or where to make donations. This tradition of the death announcement was like an obituary but more personal because you could almost feel the grief emanating from them as you stood in front of the wall where they were plastered. And as difficult as it was to see the constant reminder of your loved one's passing, I imagined it would be even harder when they were taken down and replaced by someone else's. A cruel reminder that life goes on.

As a rule, Janet didn't do funerals. She hated them and stayed as far away from them as she possibly could, refusing to go even for good friends. So it came as no surprise to me when Janet broke with some of the Italian customs. Our Italian friends and neighbors, on the other hand, were at a total loss.

First, there would be no announcements.

"I don't want to be walking through town and see the repeated proclamation of Ken's death around every corner. It would be too painful."

A part of me wanted to argue. This was how it was done here. I could picture the disapproving faces of the town elders already. But Janet was resolute.

"Ok, but how will we let people know? Shall I help you make some calls?"

La Trippa di Marinella
(serves 4 people)

- 1 kilo (2.2 pounds) of Tripe It will come already cleaned, but you can clean it again with hot water and lemon. When I did it on my own, I rinsed it two times. You can buy the tripe already cut (which I did), or you can get the disgusting looking piece of stomach and cut it yourself into strips like Marinella did!
- 1 yellow onion
- 1 carrot
- 1 celery stalk
- 1 handful of parsley
- 3 cloves of garlic
- small pieces of peperoncino (ATTENZIONE.... When I did the dish on my own I put way too much red pepper. You can't undo it once it's in. So I'd put one or two and then add more if it's not spicy enough.)
- 5 whole cloves
- Medium can of peeled whole tomatoes that you have pureed.

Chop the vegetables in a food processor and then saute in heated olive oil. Just eyeball the oil, should coat the bottom of your pot. When the vegetables are softened... Marinella made me smell the aroma of when they were just right, but if you cook them until they are softened, you will be good to go. Then add the cloves and the red pepper.

The next step is adding the tripe. Slowly add to the vegetables and stir. Add a generous amount of salt at this point and then you are a going to leave it partially covered on a low flame for almost two hours, basically until the water drains out of the tripe and then is reabsorbed.

After the two hours and the tripe has reabsorbed the water, you add the pureed tomato. Then add enough hot water to cover. Salt again.

You then let it cook slowly on a low flame for 4-5 hours. You'll know it's done because you'll see the oil rise to the top.

INVERNO /
WINTER

CHAPTER THIRTEEN

NATALE CON MARINELLA

I love the holidays. I am a card-carrying, Hallmark movie-watching, decking the crap out of my halls devotee. I would hang my stockings with care if I had any, and even in the leanest times, a real Christmas tree will grace a corner of my home. Admittedly my first Christmases in Montepulciano had not been stellar. Cinder and I had made the best of things during the meager years, but no one was happier than she when our situation improved and I was back to my Christmas-baking self and it was time to take up the mantle of sugar cookie-sampling detail once again. My girl had lost most of her hearing and slept almost all the time, but as soon as this wondrous alchemy of butter, flour, eggs, and vanilla went into the oven and the first enticing aromas drifted past her nose, she was by my side tapping her forever-long toenails like an impatient child. Most dogs would rouse for chicken or a roast, but Cinder was a sugar-cookie *appassionata*.

As November wound down and another season at the winery officially ended, I began to get excited about Christmas. I don't have the requisite ugly Christmas sweater vest or anything, but I do begin making lists and thinking about baking.

One morning I heard a commotion from Marinella's house and leaned out my window to see a crew from the Comune cutting down her huge pine tree. Apparently, she'd been serious when she said she was donating it to the town for the holidays. After they hauled it away, the change to the courtyard was unsettling, it seemed bigger but also quite naked.

Later that day when I heard Marinella calling to Ozzy, I went over to see if it might be a good time to reclaim my own Christmas tree. Cinder trailed behind me, never one to miss an opportunity to say hello to her pal Ozzy and to gaze adoringly at Marinella.

In Italy Christmas trees are sold live with the root ball so you can replant them after the holidays, and mine has always resided in a corner of Marinella's yard. This was my second one. We'd chosen it at a local nursery last December (yes, the same place where I almost had work my first year) and then stuffed it in Marinella's car for the short ride back to town. It was a petite fir, but due to Marinella's care and repotting, it had sprouted a few inches. Marinella had the greenest of thumbs and she continuously opened her garden to all of the plants I insisted on buying and then almost killed. My house was pretty much where houseplants went to die. I spotted two of my hyacinth plants she'd nursed back to life as well as a flourishing cyclamen displaying its seasonal red blooms.

"*Che fai per Natale?*" asked Marinella as we inched and scooted the tree across her courtyard by its weighty rubber pot. What are you doing for Christmas?

"I'm going to Laura and Marisa's this year for Christmas Eve." I had spent many of my last Christmas Eves with Anna and Federico's family, but Anna's dad was unwell so I'd accepted an invite to spend time with my friends at their agriturismo.

"Would you like to come to me for Christmas lunch?"

I stood up from dragging the tree to look at Marinella. Although I had spent a lot of time in her kitchen and she'd invited me over for coffee more than a few times, this was my first official invite for a holiday meal.

"*Mi piacerebbe molto,*" I said. I would love to. I hugged her, inhaling her comforting scent of tomatoes and spice, the makings of ragù, which I knew would be simmering on the stove.

She smiled and then went back to helping me get the tree through the gate so I could drag it up the street to my house.

"Good. We'll see you at 1:00."

✦   ✦   ✦

Montepulciano had caught the Christmas spirit. When I first moved to town, said spirit was in decidedly short supply, a bit meh to be honest. Aside from Antonella and a few other shopkeepers who decorated their storefronts, and the handful of white lights grudgingly strung up along the main corso around the 20th of December, there wasn't much evidence of festivity. Janet and I had begun a tradition of taking the bus up to Florence to get our Christmas fix. There we would visit the glorious tree next to the Duomo, poke our heads into shops laden with all sorts of holiday candies and confections, sip mulled wine, and return home content, feeling as if we had taken a long, glorious soak in holiday cheer.

But then came news of our own Christmas market.

You find holiday markets, *mercatini di natale*, throughout Italy, especially in the north. Some of the most famous ones are in cities like Bolzano, Verona, and Trento, where little Christmas houses form quaint village of local and handcrafted products. Rich in the scents of the season, you can feast on local specialties like grilled polenta, roasted chestnuts, and even bratwurst, while browsing in the wintry air, sipping a *vin brulé*. In Tuscany, Siena has a lovely Christmas market and the German Market next to Santa Croce in Florence is fabulous, so I was quite excited at the prospect of having one in our little town.

Janet had decided to go to England to visit friends for what would be her first Christmas without Ken, so left to my own devices, I invited my friend Starr and her kids over from Cortona to check out our holiday festivities.

I met them in the parking area near my house, otherwise known as my writing/sunbathing space.

"I like what you've done with the place," Starr said surveying the stark parking lot. I always picture you here when you say you're writing."

"Thanks. It's minimalist, but the views are great."

Starr laughed. "And you can practically wave to us in Cortona."

Starr was a recent Tuscan expat. A petite strawberry blonde, she had a ton of energy, a propensity to break into dance at any given moment, and an unhealthy attachment to the Denver Broncos. And she is perhaps the one person who has more optimism reserves than I. She and her kids, Maddy and Sam, had moved here from Colorado. Starr ran a burgeoning tour company, Travels by Starr. We had met through Tania but a shared love of wine tasting had cemented our friendship.

"Let's go!" Sam, Starr's nine-year-old, shouted impatiently and started charging up the hill bouncing a little orange ball. Maddy, 11, gave us the patented eye roll reserved for annoying younger brothers and then ran to catch up with him.

We headed up the corso in the quickly fading light of the afternoon, the kids running ahead, scarves billowing along behind them. Starr and I, veterans of scaling hill towns, followed more sedately, enjoying the twinkling strands of lights overhead and decorated poinsettias flanking the street. My contrada, Gracciano, was serving up artisanal beer from a local producer so we sipped on some pale ale and shared a paper cone of roasted chestnuts as we talked about our plans for the holidays.

Dusk was the perfect time to visit the village in Piazza Grande. As we powered up the last steep incline toward the main square, an instrumental version of "Winter Wonderland" floated in the air and the sky above the square was full of holiday images projected in lights. The town Christmas tree was particularly resplendent. Maybe because it was Marinella's tree or maybe because in prior years it had sported only a few haphazardly placed decorations, but this year it shined a little more brilliantly in the center of the square. Small wood houses were erected side by side and covered the whole of the square and along the street toward the town's *fortezza*, fort. Their stalls were laden with all things Christmas.

"Oh my gosh. If we see carolers, your Christmas spirit meter is going to go off the chart," Starr said, taking in the scene.

"And her heart grew three sizes that day!" I quipped in my best Boris Karloff imitation from *The Grinch Who Stole Christmas*.

We followed the path of the kids, who had gotten in line for hot chocolate. As always, Piazza Grande was a few degrees colder than the rest of the town because of its altitude and ever-present wind, so we tightened our scarves as we wandered the aisles of Christmas houses of treasures. Candles, cashmere, linens, local cheeses and meats, and, of course, Vino Nobile. Everything was enticingly displayed. I couldn't resist the aroma coming from a stall selling chocolate *pandoro* cakes that had been made by hand.

I spotted Antonella selling gift baskets of pasta, cookies, and jams. Her stall looked like it had been imported straight from the North Pole, and she was dressed up like Mrs. Claus. The only evidence of modernity was the space heater behind her. I introduced Starr, who bought a couple of things to take back to the States.

"Who's manning the store while you are up here all month?" I asked Antonella as she wrapped Starr's purchases.

"The kids are helping this year, but they wanted to be inside the store where it's warm," she said laughing. "*È bello qua, ma fa freddo con il vento.*" It's beautiful here, but it's cold with the wind.

Sam began tugging on Starr's arm to show her something he couldn't live without so we wished Antonella a "*Buon Natale!*" and continued on.

After a thorough wander and a few more purchases, we walked toward the fortezza where they had erected an ice-skating rink near the gardens. Outside the fort, there was a long line of harassed parents and wriggling children waiting to see *Babbo Natale* (Santa Claus). I had heard on the opening day of Santa's Workshop that the big man himself had passed out from the heat inside and had to be taken to the hospital. I wondered if he'd returned or if this was a replacement St. Nick.

The skaters at the rink all seemed to be teenagers. They bobbed and wobbled all over the ice, this obviously being a first-time experience for many of them. Christmas music had been ousted in favor of "I love it" by Icona Pop.

We strolled back down the hill and spent the rest of the evening enjoying an American feast of eggnog, tacos and cupcakes (Sam's request) and listening to Maddy and Sam laughing hysterically as we watched a Christmas movie featuring a farting reindeer. Cinder happily smushed between them on the couch, reveling in the pats and cuddles. It could have been the eggnog talking, but having friends to share in some of my Christmas traditions, and also being able to experience the Italian traditions as well, made me realize that this really had become my home. I wasn't feeling awkward or out of place anymore, trying to fit my cultural sensibility into theirs. It was beginning to blend. Maybe not seamlessly, but it was another stitch in my Christmas stocking. If I had one.

✦ ✦ ✦

On Christmas Day, I readied a plate of cookies to take to Marinella's, lobbing a sugar cookie to a grateful Cinder who had been watching me attentively. I grabbed a bottle of Poliziano Vino Nobile to bring as well. I was nervous since I had never spent time with Marinella's whole family.

The evening before at Laura's had been relaxed and enjoyable. I'd gotten to know and love her family since my first stay at their agriturismo over seven years before, so spending Christmas Eve in Marisa's kitchen brought back memories of all the wonderful hours spent there. She had prepared a traditional Italian Christmas Eve dinner of fish dishes including a scrumptious fried shrimp and cod antipasto and a risotto with calamari. Marisa is an amazing cook and I always learned a few new tricks when I watched her. At the end of the night, one of Laura's friends dressed up as *Babbo Natale* and handed out gifts to the kids. Or he tried to anyway. He had the scariest Santa Claus mask I'd ever seen, its exaggerated features and maniacal grin causing the kids to scream and cry for most his visit.

My thoughts were interrupted by Marinella's husband Nicola calling to me from outside. I looked at the clock. It was almost 1:00. I poked my head out the window.

"*Arrivo!*" I told him. I am coming.

"Leftovers later," I promised Cinder who had already snuggled back into her blanket.

I hugged Nicola as he held the gate for me, then made my way inside handing off the cookies and wine to Marinella's sister, Anna. I shrugged out of my coat trying to remember names as adults and children were introduced to me. I knew Marinella's sons Lorenzo and Giacomo already. Giacomo was our vet so I felt comfortable with him. Lorenzo didn't really say much and they'd seated me next to him so that was a bit worrying. I recognized Marinella's niece, Lucia, who had organized an English lessons group for me at Sant'Agnese the first year I was here. My red-headed student Alessio (of the uncle with the best rotisserie chicken at the market fame) had been in that first group.

I gave Marinella a hug when she finally came out of the kitchen. She had been plating an antipasto selection of crostini and salumi. She had dark circles under her eyes and appeared to be standing upright solely by an unseen force of stoic strength. I could only imagine how much an effort it had been for her to prepare Christmas lunch when she was so obviously not feeling well.

"*Sono contenta di essere qui con voi,*" I said. I am happy to be here with you. She smiled then waved me towards the table.

"*Pronti,*" she said and we all scrambled for our chairs. The room was warm and cozy, a fire burned low in the hearth and what smelled like sausages roasted over a grate.

The long table was makeshift. Three tables pushed together to hold all thirteen of us. We were stacked elbow to elbow but the mood was jovial.

As we tucked in to three different types of crostini, including my favorite *crostino nero* (a wonderful liver pâté that was typically Tuscan) and daintily cut our prosciutto and salami, Nicola asked me about New York and told me of his wish to travel there one day. Marinella wasn't fond of traveling and I glanced at her, expecting a nose wrinkle of disapproval but instead saw a melancholic expression that made the piece of *capocollo* I was chewing threaten to lodge in my throat.

At that moment one of the kids burst into song, singing a rousing rendition of the theme song to her favorite Italian cartoon, and the whole table clapped delightedly. I was grateful for the distraction and grateful to be a part of this fun-loving group.

Chatter flew at me from all directions and I tried my best to respond to questions about my work, my writing, wine, and what I'd had for dinner at Laura's the night before. Italians always seemed happiest when you recounted that you'd eaten well.

The second course of *pasta al forno* was amazing. Basically a lasagne, the Tuscans eschewed ricotta in favor of a bechamel sauce and the many creamy layers combined wonderfully with Marinella's ragù.

"*Strepitosa*," I pronounced as I savored the last bite. This was my new favorite word, which meant super delicious. Marinella beamed, then in one swift move reloaded my plate before I could protest. Had I learned nothing from the Stefano's wedding? Go slowly, and don't fill up too early.

Giacomo laughed when he saw my expression, then Marinella plopped another helping on his plate too. *Beccato*! Busted.

We both laughed.

Anna cleared plates and I was told to stay put, which was a relief since I couldn't really maneuver much except to reach my wine glass and plate.

I took advantage of Marinella being in the kitchen to ask Nicola how she was doing. "She's had a rough couple of weeks," he said softly. Sharing in this familial scene made me realize what an integral part Marinella played. With her ill, the axel that turned the wheel was faltering. When the surrounding talk turned to plans for New Year's and the usual wishes for everyone that the next year would be better than this one, Nicola raised his voice a little.

"*Non desidero niente di meglio*," Nicola said. "*Chiedo solo che il prossimo anno sia uguale a questo, non peggio*." I don't need anything better. I only ask that the next year be as good as this one, not worse.

He excused himself and went over to the fireplace, busying himself with removing the sausages and bringing them to the table. His words echoed in my head. It is often so true that we want everything to continually improve instead of really focusing on the good we already have.

Anna and Marinella reappeared with the next course, platters heaped with pieces of roasted chicken, rabbit, and pigeon. I took two small pieces and a piece of sausage and willed my stomach to accommodate this last course. A huge salad was added to the feast as well as roasted potatoes and one of Marinella's specialties, *sformato di carciofi*, which was kind of like an artichoke soufflé.

Lorenzo, who was seated on my left, had not spoken two words to me the entire meal, even when I tried to engage him in conversation. He tucked into a sausage and when the meat course was finished, he grabbed his phone and went upstairs. A hard nut to crack, that one.

Dessert included all manner of pandoro, panettone, and the platter of Christmas cookies that I'd brought. Nicola opened some chilled spumante and we spent another half hour at the table just talking, before everyone began stretching and reaching for a proffered cup of espresso. It was a perfect Christmas afternoon. Or it would be after I'd Skyped with my parents when I got home. Although we chatted every week, I missed them the most during the holidays.

When the kids began to get restless, everyone began saying their goodbyes and packing up their families. As predicted, Marinella sent me home with a little of everything. Cinder was going to love the pigeon and rabbit.

I hugged Marinella again and she walked me to the door. I thanked her for making me feel so welcome. She hugged me back and then as she always did when I got too mushy, changed the subject.

"*La prossima settimana, faccio il cinghiale se vorresti imparare la ricetta.*" Next week I am going to prepare wild boar if you want to learn the recipe. I couldn't even imagine being hungry again by then, but I didn't hesitate to answer. Time in the kitchen with Marinella was dear to me.

"*Assolutamente.*" Absolutely.

I made my way up the little hill between our houses and gave thanks for having such a wonderful friend. One thing I had come to love about my friendships here in Italy was the constant sensation of a full heart, not just a full stomach.

IN VINO VERITAS

February was my least favorite month of the year and one in which I usually crawled into hibernation. All of the holiday festivities were over and it was a month that cried out for binge-watching a new Netflix series on the couch with an aging Weimaraner and eating from boredom. Come to think of it, February was probably Cinder's favorite month. All of this while trying to stay warm in an apartment that refused to cooperate, its radiators giving off the suggestion of heat if you hovered over them but having relinquished any actual heating responsibilities many decades prior. I'd nicknamed my apartment the igloo, but this may be unfair to the igloos of the world that are most likely toasty warm inside. I spent a good portion of the cold month of February baking bread just so I could have an excuse to keep the oven on, and my students often left their parkas on when they came over for English lessons.

This particular year was different. Yes, it was still cold, but at the end of January we'd received news that the sommelier course was finally coming to Montepulciano. Suddenly I was able to shake off the winter gloom that had been descending and prepare for the opportunity to learn more about the world of wine.

In early February, Janet and I walked up the hill towards our first class in Piazza Grande with purpose. It was just after nine in the evening, and quite dark even on the main street. All of the holiday decor had been taken down and without the lights strung along the street, it felt deserted. The stores were all shut up tight. Our classes were to begin at 9:30 pm. Janet was a night owl so this was no problem for her, but I was a morning person. It was not going to be easy doing a class so late in the evening. I was glad Janet was doing it with me.

We'd gone to the presentation of the course the week before and had been surprised to see so many interested, prospective students. Palazzo del Capitano, where the course would be held, had been built in the 13th Century and there were now classrooms on the third floor. We'd been among a group of about forty people. FISAR was not prepared for the turnout and had only a handful of applications ready. I'd found a seat at the back of the room because I had been sick for about two weeks with a bronchial cough, and once it found its rhythm no amount of Halls could stop it. I'd been prepared to make a getaway if needed. We'd learned the cost of the course from a team of smartly dressed sommeliers, who gave a brief overview, and then sent us on our way.

Tonight we would get our books and the syllabus for the course. As per usual, I was a little anxious. First day of school jitters never seem to go away, do they? Whether it's kindergarten, university, or an intensive three-level sommelier course in Tuscany, that sense of nervous anticipation is always present.

Janet distracted me as we hiked up the hill, filling me in on the friends and museums she'd visited during her trip to London.

"How are you doing now that you are back?" I asked her. "Are you sure you're up to this?"

"I am. I'm grateful to have something to do. The house is too quiet." I couldn't imagine trying to pick up the pieces after a loss like she had suffered.

"Well, I am grateful we are doing this together." I linked my arm through hers as we walked. "We can help each other study for the exam."

When we arrived at the palazzo for our course and trekked up to the third floor, the place was empty. Janet had insisted on coming up early so we could get seats, but she'd obviously forgotten where we were; Italy was tough for those of us who are always pathologically early. Living here a few years had helped me a little. I still couldn't arrive after the appointed hour like many of my Italian friends, but I was working on punctual rather than early.

"Soooo, a few seats then," I said surveying the empty room. The empty, freezing room.

"*Benvenute*," said Leonardo, the course director, popping out from a little room off to the side. "Sorry about the heat. We got our wires crossed somewhere. Janet, right?" he said to me. "And Jennifer," he said to Janet. This would continue the entirety of the first level. He never could get straight who was who with these two foreign "J" names. In the end, he settled for calling us by our last names.

The room was so cold we could see our breath, and I started to feel better about the temperature that my students endured in the igloo. My house wasn't bad next to this frozen tundra, where apparently the heat hadn't been turned on since the presentation meeting the week before.

People began trickling in. Nine-thirty came and went, and it became clear that the 9:30 pm to 11:00 pm course time was not likely to happen. We were in for some long nights.

We paid our tuition monies for the first level and received our supplies. Janet wanted to sit up front. I did not, so I told her I would see her after class and found a seat a few rows back and set about looking at our new gear. My butterflies had dissipated a little, but as I unloaded the big black nylon satchel loaded with textbooks, tasting notes, corkscrew, thermometer, napkins, and four wine glasses, I realized that this was really a professional course and if we completed all three levels we would be full blown sommeliers. My teeth began chattering a little. Nerves? Or the arctic air?

My friend Federica settled into a chair next to me, bundled up with a huge scarf around her neck. She was from Torino in the north and I enjoyed her melodious accent, which was quite different from the Tuscan one I was used to hearing.

"*Pronte?*" she asked. Are we ready? In addition to the sommelier gear, she unpacked one of those graph-paper notebooks that I hated, with tiny squares instead of lines, and an *astuccio* with three sharpened pencils, a series of colored pens, and an eraser. All of my school-age students carried one of these pencil cases, but somehow Federica made it work. She looked professional and prepared.

I drew out my own brand new, spiral notebook and two pens. "*Pronta*," I replied, earning an approving look.

Leonardo asked us to go around the class and say why were taking the course. Everyone was huddled in Woolrich-style parkas or heavy coats and scarves. Feet were on their way to becoming ice blocks. Some, like me, worked in the wine profession, either at wineries or in wine shops, some were tour guides like my friend Simone who told everyone he preferred to call himself an escort, making the whole class crack up. There were two winemakers, two dentists, some farmers, and a bunch of college students. Janet and I were not the only foreigners. There were two Russians and a Colombian as well. We were a diverse group united in our love of wine.

In the first level we would learn about the production of wine, from the vineyard through fermentation and aging, and we would be tasting several wines each week from the different regions in Italy, learning not only the characteristics of the different grape varieties, but also to properly serve wine and at what temperature. Janet raised her hand a few times to ask questions and when I saw Leonardo struggling to understand her accent, I was glad I was safely a few rows back. I worried enough about my Italian without talking in front of a big class.

Some conferring was going on in the front of the class and then some bottles of bubbly were brought out.

"Bring out one of your glasses," Leonardo instructed us. "Due to the heating issues tonight, we are going to end a little early. Read the chapters in your syllabus and be prepared to open some bottles and begin serving next week."

The sommeliers began uncorking bottles and moving row to row, serving us prosecco.

Leonardo raised his glass once we were all served. "The good news is that the wine is at the perfect temperature. *Cin cin*." Cheers!

We all laughed and sipped our sparkling wine, happy that we could stand up and stamp our cold feet a bit.

+ + +

The following weeks were spent living and breathing wine. Classes were fun. We all made stupid errors. My bottle opening skills were pretty good since I did that daily at Poliziano, but I still managed an embarrassing episode when we were all given bottles to open in class. My bottle had a synthetic cork and Leonardo was next to me when I'd opened mine. I automatically raised the cork to my nose, but Leonardo caught my eye and shook his head.

"You don't smell the synthetic ones." He chuckled and leaned toward me. "*Non possono sapere di tappo se sono tappi sintetici.*" They can't be corked if they're synthetic. Erm, good point. Something I already knew but had forgotten in the heat of the moment.

I was poised to be a kick-ass sommelier.

Each week we were called to the front to open the night's tasting bottles, smell the corks, test the proper temperature of the wine, and then serve it. It was always alphabetical so Simone and I were often up at the same time. Simone was really short, but he had sexy dimples and twinkling green eyes. When he laughed you couldn't help but be charmed. His knowledge of local history was extensive, which made him a great guide. That and his excellent English. We'd met when he brought clients to the winery and I enjoyed him, but he was super sarcastic and kind of a know-it-all about everything. It gave me a teensy amount of pleasure that he was crap at opening wine bottles.

We'd dated for half a minute, but Simone preferred to play the field, so he wasn't a keeper. I'd nicknamed him Spidey after he literally tried to climb up my window when I'd refused his request for a drunken booty call. We'd both laughed as he tried repeatedly to scale the wall, calling out drunken romantic phrases. His enthusiasm was finally doused after he fell and injured himself, rolling down the incline of my building.

"*Ti sei fatto male?*" I'd called as he lay on the ground. Did you hurt yourself?

"*Sì.*" He'd limped away into the night.

Happily we'd remained friends and our ribbing in class was good-natured.

One night when I finished opening my bottles of Amarone ahead of him, Simone mumbled, "You should be good at this. You practice all the time. It's your job."

"Don't worry, Spidey. You'll get it, too."

He made a big deal of smelling the wine and as he took as a sip, I finished, "Besides, I am sure you are a great escort, you practice all the time!" I winked and he chuckled into his glass.

Opening and serving the wine took a little time to master, but the hardest part of the first level was talking about the wine. We had a chart with guidelines for visual, olfactory, and taste cues and we had to identify what we were smelling and tasting. This was challenging. I could pick out baking smells like clove and vanilla in some of the red wines, and in the whites I could identify citrus and vegetation scents – the cat pee/tomato leaf aroma of sauvignon blanc was undeniable!

Having to stand up and go through the whole chart for the wine was torturous, but little by little we began to identify a wine's acidity, tannins, and roundness. We learned how to talk about wine without defaulting to saying whether we liked it or not.

As much as I loved the wine course, the dinners and outings with some of my classmates were even more special and I adored the friendships I forged. The "back row," as Janet and I called it, was really two rows filed with the fun group: Andrea, Giulio, Irene, Guilia, and two Elenas. Four of the six would eventually become my English students. They were a tight ensemble that had known each other for years and provided the comic relief whenever we had to respond to questions in class. And they also regularly suggested going for drinks after class or an aperitivo before. I was more apt to join for a drink before class than after because it was usually after midnight before we shuffled, sometimes stumbled, home. They didn't encourage the spitting in our course so after tasting a number of wines, the lightweights among us were feeling no pain.

A colleague had given me a Pulltex wine aroma kit with 40 fragrance vials designed to help you learn the scents, so Janet and I hosted a pizza night for a small group to play and practice with the scents. Some of the back row and a couple of other friends accepted our invite.

The night of the pizza dinner, I manned the oven, spreading various toppings on the six pizzas I'd prepared so as to appeal to all tastes and then schlepped to Janet's house. I'd had dough rising all over my kitchen the whole afternoon.

"I'll tell you my mom's tip for perfect pizza," said Elena as everyone milled about Janet's kitchen, opening the wine bottles for dinner and chatting about class. "Cook it almost all the way, and then put the mozzarella on in the last five minutes."

My friend Franca's pizza recipe was pretty fabulous and it always got rave reviews, but one of the things I had come to enjoy about the Italians is that they are always ready with the cooking advice. Marinella had conditioned me for this, so I cheerfully did as Elena suggested and have been doing it ever since. It definitely raised my pizza game.

After dinner, we split up into teams, sniffing scents and refreshing our noses by smelling ground coffee from a can of Illy. But after a while we discovered that most of the scents in the super fancy Pulltex kit weren't representative of anything found in nature.

"*Fragola, sintetica*," Tiziana pronounced, a vial pressed tightly to her nose. Synthetic strawberry. And it was true. It smelled like Bubblicious chewing gum. Fake strawberry.

And from there we just got creative.

"Synthetic lemon," called out Janet. "Dishwashing soap lemon."

"*Un distributore*," said Elena. A gas station. Petroleum was what the card read. That one was pretty spot on. I couldn't wait to find that aroma in my next glass of Riesling.

Federica had the best one though. "Marijuana," she declared sending us into hysterics. I grabbed the vial. "I don't know what you've been smoking, but I think you overpaid because this is definitely eucalyptus."

We continued on for another hour, searching for the aromas in the wines we were drinking, chatting, and getting to know one another. I shared with the group my most embarrassing wine scent story. I'd been serving our dessert wine, Vin Santo, to a winery client.

"So when I describe our Vin Santo," I told them, I usually say that it has the wonderful aroma of fig (*fico*). Well on this particular day, I had an Italian client and I began to describe it the same way."

I paused as the Italians were already laughing, anticipating what was coming. "*Allora, ho detto al cliente che il nostro vin santo ha un buon profumo di fica.*" So I told the client that our Vin Santo had a lovely bouquet of vagina. Instead of fig. After a number of years here I'd been caught out with the dreaded *fico/fica* mistake!

Everyone was laughing uproariously.

I waited a beat. "The man looked at me for a moment and then slowly replied, '*Interessante*.'" Interesting.

He bought six bottles.

And on that note, our evening of pizza and *profumo* came to an end. We'd had a lot of fun, but I could *sense* that we still had some work to do before the exam.

✦   ✦   ✦

The final exam for the first level would be a written one. This was a relief because I knew to pass the third level there would be a serving component and then an oral exam. A written exam would be difficult, but less anxiety-inducing. I threw myself into Operation Pass Level 1 with zeal, and pretty much drove everyone at the winery crazy. Our winemaker had the patience of Job as he fielded all of my questions on botrytis, plant diseases, and fermentation techniques. He patiently stood with me over vines and explained how to prune them, pointing out which shoots to leave and which to cut. I must have heard the explanation ten times. My friend Andrea also tried to explain it to me. I never really did get that part.

Marinella helped me study, asking me questions off the flash cards I'd made, while I paced around her courtyard. And Janet and I had study sessions. We took every opportunity to ask each other questions like "What do you call the screw part of the wine opener?" "Why *verme*, of course." Or "What temperature should you serve a spumante?" "Four to six degrees Celsius."

On the evening of the actual exam, I didn't just have butterflies, I had a whole flock of starlings in my stomach. I was beyond nervous.

In the end, the studying and practice exams that we'd done were more than sufficient to get us through. Oh and it also helped that one of the course instructors walked around the room during the exam, offering little suggestions if we were all struggling with a question. "What are the primary scents in a Riesling?" *Albicocca* and *pesca* wafted into my ear and then floated up and down the rows like the wave at a baseball game. The apricot and peach aromas in Riesling became one of those nuggets that stuck in my head long after most of the grape varieties and DOCs from each region had started to fade.

Janet and I, and our friends from the back row, all made it through. Relief flowed over me after receiving that call from Leonardo. We gathered at our local bar to celebrate, many bottles of *franciacorta* and prosecco were passed around – naturally at a chilled four to six degrees. We toasted and cheered every time we opened a new bottle, then someone brought out a saber (as you do) and the opening of bottles with a *sciabola* commenced. Tops of bottles went flying as the saber connected, most of us taking cover as eager volunteers manifested a technique that demonstrated more enthusiasm than skill. I don't recommend trying this at home! We polished off many bottles that night in celebration.

In sommelier terms, we called this "homework" for the next level.

Fabio's Peposo

- 2 pounds beef (muscle) cut in cubes
- olive oil
- 4 cloves of garlic unpeeled, or as they say here in camicia, which is with their shirts on
- black peppercorns and ground black pepper
- Salt
- bouquet garni with a sprig of rosemary, sage and 1 bay leaf
- 1 bottle of red wine (Fabio likes to use vino nobile but the dish was traditionally done with Chianti)

In a terracotta pot, put the beef and add some good quality olive oil to massage in. Add salt and peppercorns and some ground black pepper. Cover with red wine and add the garlic cloves and herbs.

Cover pot loosely with lid or aluminum foil and cook in an oven on low heat 150 C. (300 Fahrenheit) for about four hours. The meat will be tender and falling apart. If there is still a lot of liquid you can finish it on the stove and reduce it down. Excellent with mashed potatoes or spinach.

PRIMAVERA

CHAPTER FIFTEEN

SAYING GOODBYE

Whenen Cinder and I first landed in Montepulciano we were curiosities. The townsfolk would launch long stares as us as we ambled up the cobblestoned streets. Cinder seemed undisturbed by this, but I always felt it a little unnerving. I would bust out my big American smile in response and that would just confuse them. Some even smiled back reflexively if they forgot themselves but then went right back to watching us speculatively.

But little by little the town grew used to seeing us together, the tall Americana and her leggy, gray sidekick. Cinder was one of the only female dogs in town so she never lacked for admirers even though she was already in her advancing years. She took to the attention with a Mrs. Robinson-style gusto, dancing around flirtatiously when they approached her. But if an admirer got too fresh, she would stare him down and send him scurrying behind his owner's legs.

The shopkeepers were quick to proffer a treat on our excursions so Cinder continually pulled me toward her favorite spots. Antonella could always be counted on for a bit of cheese or salami. The only place we no longer went was the pharmacy. The stern, white-coated women who worked there had never been very welcoming, but stern turned to icy disapproval one day when I popped in to pick up Cinder's arthritis medicine.

It was a busy Saturday morning, full of people waiting to pick up prescriptions or describe their ailments to the pharmacist in hope of avoiding a trip to the doctor. The older pharmacist, who was the least stern of the white coats and I think the owner, usually brought her tiny King Charles Spaniel to work. The dog would sit primly in her basket and not make a peep. Cinder had never paid it any attention.

But this day, as soon as Cinder scented the dog she immediately squatted in the middle of the pharmacy and peed. Not just a male-dog-marking his-territory-small pee, but a huge, I-am-a-female-alpha-and-don't forget-it lake of pee. The people waiting for their prescriptions had to keep hopping backward in reverse conga line formation as the lake began spreading across the pristine tile floor.

Porca miseria! It took almost a whole roll of paper towels to clean things up. People were muttering "*poverina!*" (poor thing) but I wasn't clear if they were feeling sorry for Cinder or for me. I gave the pharmacy a wide berth after that.

Cinder was also a superior judge of character and was quick to alert me to anyone who seemed off to her. She had honed this trait during our years in New York, the raised hairs on her back alerting me when we were in proximity to any number of reality-challenged people shuffling around Riverside Park. And in Italy, first with Luciana and Salvatore and then Simone, she was quick to make her disapproval known, guessing, rightly as it turned out that they didn't much care for dogs.

That spring was a sad one. Poppies were just starting to show themselves and the air was fragrant with ginestra, but I couldn't enjoy it. I knew Cinder's time with me was coming to an end. Our walks were brief and although she was still eating, I could feel that we were approaching the inevitable. Her arthritis was severe, her steps unsteady, and she'd been incontinent for over a year; at almost 15, she had lived a long life for a Weimaraner. I'd been through this already with my Labrador Miranda in New York and I remember my veterinarian telling me that I had waited too long, that she was in pain and was ready to go. I was resolute that with Cinder, when she told me it was time, I would let her go.

The tourist season had not yet begun so I spent as much time as possible with my girl, sitting in the sun just reading and being. And then came a day of panic and anxiety, of realizing that she had lost her appetite and what that meant, and then the final morning when she could no longer get up and just looked at me with big, tired eyes.

I called over to Marinella who responded immediately. She knelt on the floor next to Cinder and spoke to her soothingly in Italian. She nodded to me, and I knew it was time. I held in the rising hysteria as we called her son Giacomo who came to the house, veterinary bag in hand.

I crawled into Cinder's bed and hoisted her onto my lap as we said our goodbyes. I caressed her silky ears and thanked her for being such a good friend. And even as I told her how much I loved her and that Miranda would be waiting for her, my head was screaming "I AM NOT READY." I sobbed quietly and hugged her tight as Giacomo gave her the injections to put her to sleep forever.

And then she was gone.

My sadness was replaced briefly with anger when Giacomo prepared to take Cinder's body away for cremation. I hadn't thought about the reality of dealing with this part of it, but when Giacomo went out to his car and came back with a huge, black garbage bag, I lost it. I began bawling and may have shouted a little, all the while insisting that we carry her out in her blanket. It was cumbersome and unwieldy but I refused to let Cinder's body be taken away in a garbage bag.

I had been through it before, the loss of someone who has been a dear friend and companion and the wondering how life could possibly be the same without them in it. It is a loss that we never quite get over. And one, even as I write these words years later, that has tears flowing freely down my face. Cinder's loss was punctuated by the fact that she had come on this adventure with me. She had been a constant source of comfort during the most difficult times, and she had shared in my small triumphs as we hurdled over obstacles. I was grateful we had had such a long time together, but the house was empty without her. Even if it did still smell like her on a damp spring morning.

I was grateful when Fabio called me a few days later that it was time to get back to work. The distraction of giving tours and pouring wine helped ease the pain.

On the weekends, I would walk in our old spots and enjoy the beauty of the countryside. If Cinder had taught me anything it was that every little bit of nature needed to be sniffed and appreciated. And rolled in if you had the time.

CHAPTER SIXTEEN

THE LONG AND WINDING ROAD

Trying to avoid spending time in my empty apartment after Cinder died, I threw myself into a new challenge: getting my Italian driver's license.

Passing the driving exam in Italy is a little like winning a gold medal. People clap you on the back, they ask to see your shiny, pink permission to drive, and they boast proudly about you to their friends who haven't made it through. And I am not just talking about expats like me. Sure we are the majority of the people not passing the exam, but Italians also fail the driving test here regularly. It's not like in the States where they give you a little driving manual to study, you read it, you take the exam, and you pass the exam.

Italy has designed an exam so rigorous that most people actually pay for a driving course to help them pass the test. Then after you pass the written exam, you must take six obligatory driving lessons and have a road test before you actually win the coveted *patente*.

But wait? What about all the Italian drivers who are so crazy on the roads? Did they also have to take this test? And the answer strangely enough is yes, yes they did. At one time or another they have all gone through this rite of passage.

My first indication that getting a license in Italy was going to be different was when I was reading through the driver education manual. In addition to the universal warning about the dangers of drinking and driving, and not driving when you are overtired, there was also a clause advising that you shouldn't drive after eating hard to digest, fried, or fatty foods. *Cosa?*

By now I had of course learned that digestion was very important to the Italians. In casual conversations among friends, pizza restaurants were often rated by how easy their crust was to digest. A pizzeria deemed to have a crust that sat in your stomach like a bowling ball was doomed. I remember the flop sweat and anxiety I'd felt when I'd made pizza for the sommelier gang. When they declared it delicious, I was pleased, but when Elena commented that the dough had been leavened correctly, I beamed with pleasure.

So even though Italian friends talked about their digestive issues in the same open manner that friends in New York talked about seeing their therapists, this admonition about not eating fried foods and driving still tickled me. I went to my first class prepared for anything.

The driving school was located in a little piazza near the bus station. There was a computer store, an insurance agency, and the shop from which all the kids in town ordered their schoolbooks. It was also next door to my hair salon, so I could stop in to see Samanta and Elena before heading to class. One could only hope that the Italians gave extra points for looking good!

As I walked through the door, the harsh fluorescent lighting was startling after the foggy dark of the spring evening. A quick glance around the classroom and I immediately felt as if I'd stepped back in time to grade school. The charts, graphs, and even full-sized models of engines and car parts positioned around the room cemented the impression. Long tables with mismatched chairs huddled together, and flanking the walls sat a couple of computers, which looked as decrepit as the one Fabio and I had in our sales area.

I was the only one there. Marco, the instructor, greeted me. Tall, bald except for a goatee that was heading toward salt and pepper, and funky glasses, he was bundled up in a puffy coat and scarf despite the almost boiling temperature of the room. He explained the cost of the course and the paperwork I would need to sit for the exam. He said it all with the air of someone doing this for too many years.

I reluctantly fished out my wad of euros. I had valiantly tried to study for the written exam on my own so as to avoid the huge fees for the course, but I never made it through the practice exams successfully so it was time to bite the bullet. All told, the course costs would be over 900 euro. After the expense the sommelier course, I might have to sell a kidney. I was relieved when the instructor told me I could pay a little at a time.

"*La bella notizia è puoi continuare a venire a scuola fino a quando passi l'esame. Anche se bocci due o tre volte.*" The good news is you can continue to come to the school until you pass the exam. Even if you fail two or three times.

"Erm, *grazie.*" Was he writing me off already? Way to be encouraging, Marco.

I crab-walked between the tables, found a seat, and took out a new spiral notebook. I waited for what I assumed would be a large class of teenagers eager to get out on the road.

Instead there was only one woman from Poland who didn't speak much Italian, and a 20-year-old Italian girl who informed me that she'd been coming for three months and still didn't feel ready to take the exam. As the weeks went on, a few more people joined us, including one young kid who wanted to drive a scooter.

For all of us, having a license would open up our world. For me it meant not having to take the bus to work. A 10-minute ride by car turned into almost an hour commute on the bus with stops, a meandering route through the Tuscan countryside, and then a 10-minute walk from Montepulciano Stazione to the winery. Willie Nelson's "On the Road Again" became my theme song.

It wasn't that the bus was horrible. The bus drivers on my route were amusing and over time I got to know them all since I was usually the only passenger on the route. When they learned I was doing the driving exam, they joked that they wouldn't have any passengers left. Massimo and Giuliano were my favorite *autisti* (drivers). We had chats about current cinema, wine, and music and they were both really funny. Plus, they often drove me directly to the winery if it was raining to save me getting soaked by drivers splashing me on the narrow road.

So the real trick to passing the driving exam was just to show up for lessons.

Marco had a computer at the front of the class and he used a program that demonstrated the topic for the evening. I took loads of notes, trying to memorize the ridiculous amount of road signs, insurance rules, and the various types of licenses, which corresponded with vehicles depending on how many cylinders they had.

But my nemesis was figuring out who had the *precedenza*, or right of way. It wasn't a straightforward car on the right goes first rule like I was used to. Nope. Instead there were scenarios. Lots and lots of scenarios. Was there a stop sign at the intersection? Yield? Was one of the vehicles a bus? What about horses? The number of scenarios proffered made me feel like I was being gaslighted, as every time I was sure I had it figured out, the Charles Boyer of Italian question construction was ready with another variation to help me lose my sanity.

The Polish lady and the young girl didn't really get it either so I just concentrated on things I was able to memorize, like if someone was injured in an accident and had fractured something not to give them water and that shock victims needed to be laid on the ground with their feet in the air.

I had a few moments during the month of classes when I tried to convince myself that the bus wasn't so bad, but then Willie Nelson would start crooning in my ear and I would resolve to push on. After a month of lessons and doing practice exams three or four times a day, I was getting just one or two wrong on each exam and that was usually just a sneakily worded question. I came to admire the art of the double negative and the archaic Italian words peppered throughout the exams. There were over 7,000 possible questions so there was no memorizing possible. As soon as you tried that, the next time you saw the question a "can" would be changed to "can't" and you were screwed if you didn't catch it. Four errors was passing; five, you failed.

When I was ready to book the actual exam, I had to get a doctor's note saying that I was in good health and have an eye exam. Then Marco scheduled the date. It would be in Siena and Marco would drive.

On exam day those of us taking the test, which was just me and Scooter Boy, piled into the driving school's blue Fiat Panda and tried to act confident. Marco gave us a pep talk and reminded us not to get tripped up by the three different types of railroad crossings.

The examination room in Siena was filled with aisle upon aisle of computer monitors. Unlike the computers we had practiced on, these were touch screen.

A no-nonsense proctor with a tight perm called out our names and told us where to sit. She went over a few rules and admonished us to turn off our cell phones. If a cell phone rang during the exam, we all failed automatically. She showed us how to login with our computer screen.

I kept touching mine but nothing happened. I caught the proctor's eye, and she frowned in my direction.

"*Signora, deve spingere la scelta.*" Madam, you must push the choice."

My face flamed red as 30 people turned in their seats to stare at me.

"*Sto provando, ma non si muove.*" I'm trying but it's not moving. I tried for a laugh. "*Scusa la straniera che fa casino.*" Excuse the foreigner who is making a disturbance. A small chuckle drifted from the other side of the room.

The proctor walked over and stood over me like an impatient parent, tapping at the screen until I was on the same page as the rest of the group.

The test loaded, I took a deep breath and then settled in. I had time to go back through twice before the time was up.

We were sent out of the room for 10 minutes and then called back in for the results. At least half were failing. "*Bocciata,*" a young girl said, sniffling into her phone.

I heard my name and walked up to the proctor.

"*Ha superato,*" she told me. "*0 errori.*" She smiled at me.

I'd passed and I hadn't missed one!

I looked around for Scooter Boy. He'd passed, too. We both hugged Marco with joy and relief. One hurdle down. Now on to the driving.

✦　　✦　　✦

When the little blue Fiat pulled up to the tourist parking lot outside Montepulciano's gate, I was ready.

"*Pronti?*" Marco said echoing my thoughts as he loped around from the driver's side to get in on the passenger side. "Are we ready?"

"*Certo.*" Sure. "I did just eat an entire *bistecca alla fiorentina* but I am sure it will be fine."

Marco laughed. I joked to cover my nervousness. The large print SCUOLA GUIDA emblazoned on the back of the car didn't help. I had driven infrequently in the last 10 years since I hadn't had a car in New York or here. Other than a few short stints with visiting friends in their rental cars, and one or two with Marinella, I hadn't really driven. And I hadn't owned a car with a stick shift in over 15 years.

I took a deep breath and channeled my inner Bette Davis. Fasten your seat belts, it's going to be a bumpy ride.

It wasn't so bad. We drove to Chianciano about 10 minutes away. That was the town where we would do the road test. I didn't stall once and Marco didn't have to employ his footbrake. He actually looked super relaxed as he always did which made me wonder if he was a pot smoker or just inured from years of putting his life in the hands of eager adolescent drivers.

The only thing that Marco had to tell me repeatedly was to not rest my hand on the gear shift.

"Just do like the nuns, and slap my hand if I do it again," I suggested.

The admonition about keeping my hands on the wheel brought back memories of my first driving testing in Vermont when I was 16 years old. I'd learned to drive on my parents' Subaru, which was a stick shift, but I'd decided for the driving exam to use their Lincoln Continental because it was an automatic.

The test had gone well. I executed a perfect three-point turn, and the hill stop was no problem in the automatic. I parallel parked with confidence and then when I was in the spot, I looked over at the instructor and smiled widely.

He looked at me curiously, not sure what the heck I was smiling about. "If you can get yourself out of this, we can go on, otherwise you'll have to retake the test."

When I just sat there staring at him blankly, unsure what the heck I had done wrong, he was kind. "You're on the curb." WHAT? With my parents' huge tank of a car I hadn't even noticed.

Parallel parking on the mean streets of Chianciano Terme was straightforward. Other than trying to remember Marco's very specific and precise rules in Italian, it was doable. I always managed to get the car in the spot even if it wasn't pretty.

The hardest parts of driving in Italy were the hill stops and the multitude of crosswalks to contend with in Chianciano. It was a community of walkers and if you failed to stop for someone you automatically failed. It was made more challenging by vehicles blocking crosswalks so you couldn't really see until you were right up on it if there was someone waiting to cross. It was like a game of Frogger with elderly pedestrians darting into crosswalks at any given moment.

"If that had been the actual exam you would have failed," Marco was fond of telling me as I drove past a crosswalk with a woman in a walker slowly inching toward it.

"She was just crosswalk adjacent," I'd argued. "She hadn't really decided if she was going to cross or not." Marco chuckled.

At least none of the crosswalks were on hills. I'd been taught to use the hand break on steep inclines and to let it out slowly. This apparently wasn't done in Italy so I would have to learn to "trust in the clutch," that elusive feathering of the clutch that once mastered became second nature, but when you were actually thinking about it became impossible to do without revving the engine like a starter at NASCAR.

After our six hours of lessons over the course of a month, I felt ready for my road test and Marco scheduled it for the following week.

The actual test took 10 minutes. The examiner I guess realized I could drive and had me drive around a bit and then back into a parking space. No parallel parking, no hill stop. She handed me my license and that was it. After three months and a fortune in euro, it was rather anticlimactic.

I was nevertheless ecstatic and shouted the news far and wide. Italy doesn't make things easy, but when you succeed it sure feels good.

Now I just needed to get a car.

CHAPTER SEVENTEEN

LEZIONI DI VITA

It was a cold and sunny Saturday. I opened the kitchen window, duvet cover in hand, debating whether I should hang out my laundry. Despite an early spring, winter had tiptoed back in and a thick fog swirled below the town, Montepulciano an island floating above it.

Marinella was at her laundry room window leaving food for the cats. She had a new one named Bandito but he wasn't allowed to come inside. Nicola had apparently finally put his foot down on the number of feline boarders they housed. Bandito came running when he heard the kibble hit the bowl.

Marinella saw my intention with the duvet and gave me a quick finger wag.

"*Arriva anche qua.*" It's coming here, too. She pointed to the fog. As she spoke, tendrils of precipitation insidiously swirled their way toward us, and the sunny sky slowly disappeared.

She was right, as always.

"*Ma che fai? Vieni da me. Facciamo la trippa.*" What are you doing? Come over, we'll make tripe."

"Erm, ok. *Va bene.*"

Many people might be a little squeamish about cooking cow stomach, but any opportunity to learn from Marinella was precious to me. Yes, I would have been more excited if she had said we were making ravioli or roasted *nana* (duck), but I hung my laundry on a drying rack, grabbed my cooking notebook, and hurried over.

When I entered Marinella's kitchen I felt my shoulders lower, releasing a tension I hadn't realized I'd been holding. I disliked being in my apartment without Cinder. It was lonely and it was sad. The warmth of Marinella's kitchen, with Ozzy and the cats making their usual chaos, was just the tonic I needed.

Marinella had the coffee going already, the scent of the percolating brew from the *moka* enveloped us in its warmth. She was dressed in what I always thought of as her cooking uniform, a red hoodie, topped by a faded red apron with peppermint swirls on it. I knew she had an extra pair of reading glasses in the apron's front pocket. She seemed thinner to me, tired and fragile. She had fallen twice in the last couple of weeks.

We sipped our espresso and Marinella began laying out the basic recipe for me. We were there to cook tripe, but we were doing much more. We were silently acknowledging that if we wanted to preserve recipes for memoriam this was the time to do it. I forced myself to be present in the moment and not think about the future.

I stood at the table and rough chopped carrots, onion, celery, and garlic. Meanwhile, Marinella washed the cow stomach in two changes of hot water and lemon, then cut it into strips. It was already clean, she told me, but it was always good to clean it again. No argument here.

"*Allora, hai trovato un fidanzato?*" Have you found a boyfriend? She took the chopped vegetables and added them to a pot of heated oil.

"No, *nessuno.*"

"*Che fine ha fatto a Spider-Man?*" What happened to Spider-Man?

We both laughed. Normally I wouldn't have told Marinella about Simone's antics because it was embarrassing, but she had heard him trying to crawl up my window in his drunken ardor.

"*Hai bisogno di un bravo uomo,*" she told me, "*non solo uno che tromba bene.*" You need a good man, not just one who is good in bed.

Again, no argument here. The beautiful men abound in Italy but finding a keeper seemed beyond my skill set.

Marinella cooked the vegetables until they began to soften and then added a couple of pieces of *peperoncino.* Then she took out a little jar and counted out five cloves.

"*Il segreto*," she whispered, holding up the cloves. The secret to her tripe.

The familiar scent of clove wafted up from the pot, instantly reminding me of baked ham, and pomander balls, the oranges my mom always decorated for Christmas then rolled in spices.

We added the tripe to the pot with some salt. It needed to cook for about two hours before we added chopped tomatoes. Any other day, I might have gone home in between, but today for some reason, I didn't. Instead, we talked about everything. Just like we always did on our walks. We talked about going asparagus hunting in another week, how this year we would get there first. We cleaned artichokes and talked about our neighbors. Marinella asked how Janet was doing without Ken. Mrs. Hobbs, she still called her, even though they had been neighbors for 20 years. We talked about Marinella's upcoming surgery to remove a small tumor, the culprit causing her to lose her balance. It was benign but needed to come out. We talked, and shared, and cooked.

We sampled *la trippa*. The sauce was tasty, but I was not a fan of the consistency of the tripe. However, if someone held a gun to my head, I would be able to cook it.

"*Buona*," I declared. It's good.

Marinella laughed. "*Non piace a tutti.*" Not everyone likes it. "*Ma ora hai molte ricette toscane che puoi cucinare per la tua famiglia un giorno.*" But now you have many Tuscan recipes you can make for your family one day.

I was on the verge of becoming emotional so I just hugged her, trying to will some of my strength into her thin frame. She hugged me back and I felt so grateful for all of her guidance and friendship.

That day was one of those rare moments in time that stay with you and that you can replay over and over again when you need to be reminded of the good. It had been a day of laughter, friendship, and . . . well, cow stomach.

✦   ✦   ✦

Less than a week later, I was awakened by an early morning phone call from Nicola.

"*Ho una brutta notizia. Marinella ci sta lasciando,*" he told me. His voice cracked on the last word. His bad news was that Marinella was leaving us.

What? No no no. She had gone in for the surgery and everything had been fine. She'd been alert after they removed the tumor. But apparently she was not fine. Her cancer-ravaged body had not been strong enough to hold on. She slipped into a coma and a few days later, the doctors declared her legally dead.

Even as I took care of Ozzy and the cats while Nicola and the boys camped out at the hospital in Siena, I still refused to believe it was true. It seemed impossible to me that someone as full of life as Marinella could be gone from this world.

Ozzy was beside himself, sensing that something was terribly wrong. He actually bit me when I tried to take off his leash one morning. I had on a coat so he didn't break the skin, but I choked back a sob because I knew how upset he was. I wished Cinder had been with us, she could have at least comforted him a little. He refused every treat I tried to give him, instead spending his time restlessly pacing the garden. Even in the months that followed, Ozzy would sit vigil at the gate waiting for Marinella to come home.

They brought Marinella's body back to Montepulciano and at the hospital, in a viewing room across the hall from where I had said goodbye to Ken, I stood over my friend's body and said goodbye to her. She looked so peaceful. I cried unashamedly. I hugged Nicola and Giacomo, wanting to comfort them, but really they had comforted me. Even Lorenzo let me hug him.

What would they do without her? She had been the rock of their family.

The funeral was held at Sant'Agnese. As I walked over to the church, my attention was drawn to the *rondini* flying and swooping up near the belltower. The swallows had returned, as they always did in the spring. It was comforting to see them, even though in that moment it was a heartbreaking reminder that life continues on even when we feel like everything has stopped.

While the nave of Sant'Agnese was much larger than the church where Stefano had gotten married, just like on that day, the place was packed. I had to squeeze along an aisle just to be able to see the proceedings. Marinella had never been very religious but I think she would have liked the service. The priest talked about her long battle with cancer and how much a part of the community she was and how much she would be missed. And then members of our contrada filed in, some garbed in full medieval dress and carrying flags, and some wearing their Gracciano colors, their black and green scarves with the image of the lion. The drummers beat their familiar tune, which during the summer had heralded the joy of the Bravio, but now managed to somehow capture the mournful mood of the congregation.

Seeing the contrada come out to pay their last respects to Marinella made it sink home how beloved she was by the whole community. It was a small moment of light during the saddest days after her death and one that made my heart a little less constricted every time I thought of it.

I made my way out of the Church drained and at loose ends. When I crossed the street, I saw Janet waiting for me. She hadn't been at the service, but she silently linked arms with me and walked me home.

CHAPTER EIGHTEEN

TO EVERYTHING
THERE IS A SEASON

I'll admit to floundering a little after the loss of Marinella. Every time I glanced at her forlorn garden through my window, a wave of sadness washed over me. Terracotta pots sat empty and the whole aspect of the garden was one of neglect. Who would take care of it now? Nicola and the boys didn't have the time or inclination to give it the love and attention that Marinella had.

Have you ever had those moments after someone close to you dies where you think you see them? It happened to me once about a month after Marinella's death. I was walking toward the mercato and saw a woman with the same hair, the same silhouette, and from the back it was her. A moment of elation swept through me, followed swiftly by sadness when my brain caught up and reminded me it couldn't possibly be her.

And I had to admit Janet was right about the death announcements posted throughout the town. It was awful walking along and coming upon one unexpectedly, a sharp jab to the heart every time I saw Marinella's notice looming down from one of the walls of the town. And as I had suspected, it was even sadder when it was taken down.

On the weekends I made ragù and practiced my pasta-making skills. I often brought ragù over to Nicola and the boys, hoping it would comfort them as much as it had comforted me cooking it. I continued my routine of walking in the rolling countryside outside of town where I felt closest to my dearest companions. Marinella was there in the fragrant perfume of the ginestra and in the colorful bloom of the poppies, and Cinder was there in the tall green grasses and the flowers of the olive trees.

The winery kept me occupied and one morning as I entered our tasting room, I heard raised voices coming from the kitchen. Fabio and our caterer Massimiliano were having a spirited discussion as to whether it was too late in the season to make *peposo*. It was a traditional Tuscan dish, basically a delicious beef stew with black pepper that was cooked under wine for hours in the oven. It was one of my favorites and Fabio's signature dish.

"*É un piatto invernale*," insisted Massimiliano. "*Non si fa in primavera*." It's a winter dish. You don't make it in the spring.

"*Hai ragione, ma devo preparare un piatto caldo per un gruppo grande*." You are right, but I need a hot dish I can make for a large group.

The group in question was coming with our Swiss importer, Zanini, who had been with the winery for a long time. In my first year at Poliziano, I had gained some legendary status for an enormous faux pas involving Zanini, in fact. One morning as I was vacuuming the tasting room and getting ready for the day, a distinguished looking man walked in and said, "*Buongiorno*. I am your Swiss importer." So I promptly smiled and, feeling rather pleased with myself, said, "Oh, Zanini."

The man glared at me for a beat and then walked toward the offices. "Your other Swiss importer." Oops. How was I to know we had two? And how was I to know they apparently hated each other?

Fabio had come rushing in and told me everyone was in an uproar because I'd insulted the importer.

"I can't have caused an international incident," I joked. "They're Swiss. They are above such things."

Fabio tried to hide a smile. "Just stay out of the office today."

"So our Swiss importer is coming, I hear," I said as I entered the kitchen and into the food discussion war. "I guess that means I won't be needed to work that evening."

"Ha, good try," Fabio laughed. Massimiliano said nothing but watched me with his twinkling eyes and mischievous grin from where he was seated at our worktable. Finally, he sipped his espresso and said, "*Ciao, Americana.*"

Massimiliano had asked me out a couple of times, but I hadn't said yes. Although he had supposedly broken up with his girlfriend, I knew he hadn't extricated himself completely. Rumors were that they were breaking things off for good, but until that happened I wasn't biting. I'd been down that road before. I'd told him to call me when he was free.

"So what's on the menu?" I asked, feigning innocence as I'd already overheard their seasonal discussion. And then I made myself scarce as their voices became animated again. You gotta love Italians and their passion for food.

The fact that Fabio was willing to make a dish that was out of season delighted me. Maybe I was rubbing off on him. As much as I felt like my roots were now fixed, and I was becoming a part of the culture here, I was essentially a dish out of season. The basic ingredients were there to make a respectable Italian, but whether it was my accent and struggle with the *congiuntivo*, or my refusal to believe in *colpo d'aria (Many Italians believed you would get sick just by a change in air temperature)*, or even the way I folded my towels, I would always be American.

In the beginning this bothered me. I was so concerned with fitting in that I tried to mold myself into the perfect Italian. I'd been self-conscious about the way I set a table, or what I should order in a restaurant, or how I prepared a plate of pasta. I didn't want my Americanness to identify me, to be one of those expats who come to live in a country without learning the language and without really trying to be a part of the community. But slowly, as I learned the language and became a part of the community, I realized that it was also okay to just be me: to laugh at the cultural differences like my ongoing struggle with hanging out the laundry, or going outside with wet hair without catching pneumonia, to be somewhat eccentric, like drinking a glass of wine in the parking lot beside my big ole dog, and even to embrace the things that I would never master. Like the tablecloth fold.

As if on cue, Fabio came in wielding a humongous green tablecloth to set up for a lunch group with our culinary tour friends, Giovanni and Sharon. It was of constant amusement to Fabio that I could never quite finesse the tablecloth fold. The tablecloths were ridiculously too long for the tables and required doubling each time we used them. I never managed to do it without exasperating Fabio. Did I mention he's a Virgo? A perfectionist if ever there was one.

To his credit he still tried. I studiously folded and met him in the middle in our tablecloth ballet.

"*Tira, tira*," Fabio ordered. Pull, pull. I obediently pulled but apparently not to his satisfaction. Fabio glared at me as my shoulders shook and I began to giggle.

"The tomatoes you cut like an expert now, the cheese slices look less like a doorstop, but the tablecloth, *mai mai mai*?"

"Never never never," I repeated in English with a laugh. "You went to school for this," I told him. This was my usual rebuttal since he had studied hotel and restaurant management.

"Yes, because you must go to school to learn to fold a tablecloth. *Madonna Americana!*" I was ridiculously pleased that Fabio had invented an Italian curse word just for me.

"Face it, Frisky, if I start to do everything perfectly you will have nothing to criticize and feel superior about. Then what will you do?"

"*É vero,*" he said with an exaggerated nod. It's true. He handed me the ends of the tablecloth again. "Let's try it again."

"You know we could solve this problem by buying tablecloths that fit the tables. Just saying." Fabio tried to look serious but I knew he was on the verge of laughing too.

You could take the girl out of the States, but not the States out of the girl. That was me, a delicious dish, served slightly out of season.

When our last group had gone and I'd loaded the wine glasses into the dishwasher, I stepped out of the kitchen into the vineyard. The sun was lowering in the sky and the vineyards looked as if they were on fire. The grapes on the vine were still green, but the bunches were growing. Another season was well underway.

I breathed in the fragrant air that was starting to cool. As always, I was comforted by the continuity of the changing seasons, knowing that spring would always bring the rebirth and regrowth that we so needed after the starkness of winter. And that summer would provide the fruits and bounty we would enjoy into the autumn. Each year I looked forward to experiencing these rhythms.

Fabio wandered out, munching a hunk of bread that he had smushed together with some prosciutto.

"Are you thinking of your friend?" he asked putting an arm around my shoulder.

"Yes, of Marinella and of the changing seasons. Life can be so fleeting, but then I look at these vines which have put down deep roots and they manage to reproduce year after year. It's reassuring."

"You know what else we can always count on, Criswell?"

"What's that, Frisky?"

"We will always have wine glasses to dry. Come on, let's get it done."

I laughed and followed Fabio back inside. "Way to ruin my philosophical moment."

Fabio winked and tossed some paper towels my way. He started humming what sounded like *Circle of Life* from the Lion King.

I groaned. "It's going to be a looooong season."

EPILOGUE

Another season passed, and before long I was contemplating a bigger change. The next year found me moving to the countryside, not in Montepulciano as I had originally thought, but a half hour down the road in Cortona closer to my expat friends Tania and Starr.

Thanks to Federico advancing me some of my salary, I had been able to get a car. Having a car had opened up possibilities for me and while it was a longer commute to Poliziano, I needed a change. Montepulciano just wasn't the same for me without Marinella. I felt her loss keenly and I couldn't take looking out my kitchen window, or sitting in the parking area, and seeing her desolate garden.

While spending a weekend at Tania's, I'd stumbled upon the sweetest little apartment in the countryside, and I just knew. It was perfect for me. Finally, I had my garden. Tania's dad cut a few Poliziano wine barrels in half for me and I used them to plant tomatoes, cucumbers, and herbs, yes even cilantro. I also planted a lavender bush so I could always hear Marinella telling me when it was getting unruly.

In the summer I invited friends from Montepulciano and Cortona to a Ferragosto barbecue and happily cooked ribs, potato salad, and carrot cake for both Italians and expats. I was particularly glad to see Janet and my pals from the sommelier course. Everyone contributed something. Plates with prosciutto and melon, bruschetta, and *panzanella* sat side by side with corn bread, guacamole, and deviled eggs. This blending of cultures seemed a perfect metaphor for my life here in Tuscany.

That winter, my friend Mirco gave me one of his German Shorthaired Pointer puppies and I named her Syrah for the wine of my new town. On one of my first walks in the countryside with the puppy, I unclipped her leash and let her run ahead on the frozen February terrain. The winter wheat had been planted and vibrant green sprouts were emerging in the fields abutting our path.

Syrah stopped and sniffed something in the short grasses and then laid down and rolled. I burst out laughing even though I was sure it was something gross. I felt Cinder's presence in that moment and knew she would approve. I savored the moment and let the winter sun warm me. With each passing day and season, Tuscany continued to inspire and fulfill me. I didn't know what my next chapter would be, but I couldn't wait to find out.

ACKNOWLEDGEMENTS

My time in Italy has been an adventure. And as with any adventure, there have been many people who have been integral to the journey and I would like to thank them here.

My Mom and Dad, who share my love of Italy and who have been my unflagging cheerleaders.

Fabio, not only the best coworker a person could have, but a true friend.

The Carletti Family who nurtured my passion for great wine.

Sherrie, Anu, and Ruth for volunteering to be advance readers, and giving me invaluable input.

Janet, for always being there.

And Kari Hock and Michelle Kaminsky for making *At Least You're in Tuscany* a reality, and for believing in this continuing tale.

JENNIFER CRISWELL is a lawyer-turned-writer who moved to Tuscany in 2009 after a life-changing trip to Italy. Jennifer lives and writes in a small hill town in Tuscany with her crazy but lovable German Shorthaired Pointer, Syrah.

Printed in Great Britain
by Amazon

84399706R00096